Ireland

Ireland

LAND OF THE CELTS

IAIN ZACZEK

COLLINS & BROWN

First published in Great Britain in 2000
by Collins & Brown Ltd
London House
Great Eastern Wharf
Parkgate Road
London SW11 4NQ

Distributed in the United States and Canada by
Sterling Publishing Co., 387 Park Avenue South, New York, NY 10016, USA

1 3 5 7 9 8 6 4 2

British Library Cataloguing-in-Publication Data:
A catalogue record for this book is available from the British Library.

ISBN 1 85585 765 0

Editorial Director: Sarah Hoggett
Editor: Mandy Greenfield
Picture Researcher: Liz Moore
Designed by: The Bridgewater Book Company

Reproduction by: Classic Scan Pte Ltd, Singapore
Printed and bound in Italy by G. Canale & C. S.p.A. - Turin

Half-title: Detail of Celtic style brooch
Title page: Ornamental page from the *Book of Kells*
Contents page: Blasket Islands, County Kerry

CONTENTS

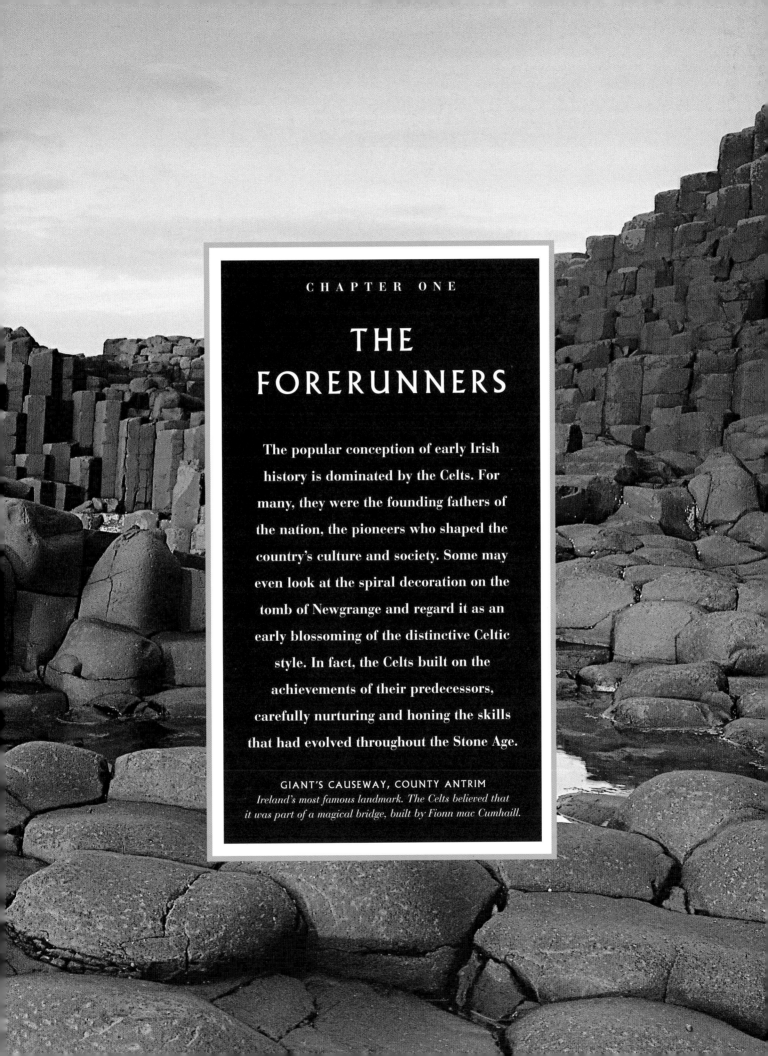

CHAPTER ONE

THE FORERUNNERS

The popular conception of early Irish history is dominated by the Celts. For many, they were the founding fathers of the nation, the pioneers who shaped the country's culture and society. Some may even look at the spiral decoration on the tomb of Newgrange and regard it as an early blossoming of the distinctive Celtic style. In fact, the Celts built on the achievements of their predecessors, carefully nurturing and honing the skills that had evolved throughout the Stone Age.

GIANT'S CAUSEWAY, COUNTY ANTRIM
Ireland's most famous landmark. The Celts believed that it was part of a magical bridge, built by Fionn mac Cumhaill.

THE FORERUNNERS

IRELAND'S EARLIEST HISTORY was determined by the forces of nature, rather than by people. There was no human habitation before the end of the Pleistocene era, which corresponded with the last Ice Age. Throughout this inhospitable period the climate fluctuated, but during the interglacials (the warmer interludes), some plant and animal life managed to prosper. Remains of reindeer, bears, mammoths, Arctic foxes and even a spotted hyena have all been unearthed from various caves or lowland sites.

The ice finally retreated around 8300 BC. The new climate, which was designated the Pre-Boreal phase, was still extremely cold, but it enabled birch, aspen and heather to grow. Some fauna may also have crossed over a temporary land-bridge which linked Antrim to the west coast of Scotland. The earliest signs of human life are much harder to determine. Archaeologists have uncovered a number of Palaeolithic artefacts on Irish soil, but none of these offers definitive proof of native life. The problem is typified by the tiny flint axe that was discovered at the promontory fort of Dun Aenghus, in County Galway. Experts agree that it dates from the Middle or Upper Palaeolithic era, but are convinced that it was washed on to its Irish find-spot from elsewhere.

The First Inhabitants of Ireland

Instead, the first traces of human activity in Ireland are assigned to the Mesolithic or Middle Stone Age. These people have been broadly categorized as 'Larnian', taking their name from Larne in County Antrim, where particularly impressive finds have been made, chiefly implements of flint, the only material durable enough to have survived down the ages. These included scrapers, blades, axeheads and leaf-shaped flakes (asymmetrical, three-dimensional lozenges with an elongated upper half). Such tools differed markedly from comparable artefacts elsewhere in Europe, suggesting that there were no contacts with neighbouring communities at this time.

The remains of several Early Mesolithic settlements have been excavated, with the most detailed studies taking place at Mount Sandel, County Derry. Here, traces were found of a number of circular huts, each with their own central hearth for cooking. Nearby there were various pits, which may have been used for storage purposes, and an 'industrial' area where the flint tools were manufactured. At this particular site, the favourite implement was a narrow-bladed microlith (tiny stone), several hundred of which were discovered in the pits. The area also featured substantial food middens, containing the bones of

small animals, birds, eels and salmon, together with the husks of hazelnuts and seeds. Radiocarbon tests on the nutshells produced dates that ranged from 8960 +/- 70 BP (Before Present) to 8440 +/- 65 BP. The variety of the foodstuffs also suggested that Mount Sandel may have been a permanent base, unlike the other known Mesolithic sites, which were seasonal.

Mesolithic people were hunter-gatherers, but prior to 3000 BC a new culture made its appearance in parts of Ireland. This was based round farmers, who raised crops and kept domesticated animals. They probably originated in Britain, bringing with them the skill of making pottery and different burial customs, although it is also possible that the changes were made by the indigenous population as a result of increasing contacts with the outside world. Either way, the change was gradual and there was a considerable degree of overlap between the Mesolithic and Neolithic (New Stone Age) lifestyles.

Clearing the Land

The principal evidence for the new farming methods revolves around the process of land clearance or *landnam* ('land taking'). Studies at a number of Irish sites have shown that, shortly after the start of the Sub-Boreal phase the classic *landnam* pattern began to take shape. Large areas of woodland were cleared by the new farmers, followed by the planting of cereal crops and, ultimately, the

OSSIAN'S GRAVE, COUNTY ANTRIM
Ancient burial sites were often named after Celtic heroes. This court cairn commemorates Ossian, son of Fionn, one of the leading warriors of the Fianna.

gradual reappearance of the forest. Flora varied from site to site, but the principal casualty of the clearance stage was undoubtedly the elm tree. Farming activity is indicated by the pollen of ribwort plantain – a weed that is associated with organized cultivation practices – along with sorrel and nettles. As the forest grew again, these began to disappear.

The decline of the elm was a widespread phenomenon which affected many parts of Europe. Archaeologists

used to regard it as the dividing line between the Mesolithic and Neolithic epochs. Recently, however, a note of caution has been introduced. Elm shoots would have provided the ideal fodder for domesticated cattle, and it may be that the trees suffered unduly from the development of animal husbandry. The ravages of Dutch elm disease, which proved such a problem in the latter part of the twentieth century, have also encouraged speculation that there had been a similar blight in prehistoric times.

The clearance of forests required a new and sturdier type of tool to enable the settlers to fell trees. Experiments have shown that polished stone axes were ideal for this task. In Ireland, the two principal centres of axe

LOUGH GUR, COUNTY LIMERICK
This segment of a stone circle comes from one of Ireland's most mystical sites. The nearby lake is said to be one of the portals of Tir na nOg.

production were at Tievebulliagh and Brockley, both in County Antrim. The former, in particular, must have established some sort of reputation, because its products have been found throughout Ireland and Britain, on sites as far afield as Cornwall, Kent and Aberdeenshire. Undoubtedly the stone-workers chose Tievebulliagh because of its rich supply of porcellanite, a durable, jasper-like shale. Rough blocks of this material were shaped by the stone-workers through chipping and transverse flaking, before being polished and fitted into curved wooden hafts. In addition to their distinctive axes, the workers at Tievebulliagh also produced tools such as stone chisels and adzes – the former possibly for tilling the soil; the latter for woodworking.

Neolithic Pottery

Pottery appears to have been an innovation of the New Stone Age – no trace of it having as yet been discovered on Mesolithic sites. The blanket term for this ware is Western Neolithic, although it has been broken down into a host of local, specialized forms. The earliest examples seem to have been plain, round-bottomed bowls, swiftly followed by flat-based varieties. In general, the most distinctive feature created by Irish potters from this period was the pronounced 'shoulder' on their vessels.

Pottery types are usually named after the original find-spots of good, representative items. Among the more prominent types are the Dunmurry style, which owes its

LOUGH GUR

The Neolithic settlements at Lough Gur may no longer have appeared particularly impressive by the time the Celts arrived, but hints of the importance of the site lingered on in folk memory. The newcomers fostered the belief that the place was under the protection of Anu, their mother goddess, and from that time on Lough Gur became the focus of scores of local superstitions. Many regarded it as an enchanted place, believing that it was dangerous to sit by its banks or even to gaze for too long at its waters. 'The old people used to say that the sky was widest over Lough Gur,' declared one local, adding mysteriously, 'My own father always told me that it wasn't right to be out late at night in the hills around here. He said we'd get some kind of fairying out of it.'

According to superstition, Anu was said to materialize in or near the lake. Sometimes she took the form of an old woman, sometimes a young girl and sometimes a mermaid. Her most terrifying appearance is deemed to have occurred in 1938, when excavation work was taking place at one of the Neolithic tombs, nicknamed the Giant's Grave. Appalled by this act of desecration, the goddess gathered together her banshees (the *Bean Sidhe* or 'women of the fairy mounds') and howled all night long around the shores of Lough Gur.

name to a hearth site in County Antrim; Lough Gur Class I and Class II ware (the distinction being the shape of the base), which is most notable for the vessels from Rockbarton and Kilhoyle; Carrowkeel ware (named after a cemetery in County Sligo), which is recognizable by its stab-and-drag decoration; and Sandhills ware, which takes its name from a series of sites in north-eastern Ireland that have yielded up a rich variety of Neolithic pottery, much of it featuring heavy club-rims and bird-bone ornamentation.

Pottery of this kind has been unearthed at both domestic and burial sites, but the latter – being designed as permanent structures – have yielded up a far greater profusion of finds. The farming and pastoral peoples of the Western Neolithic Zone (a division of Early/Middle Neolithic cultures) developed distinctive funerary patterns on their pottery. They showed a preference for communal burials, whether using cremation or inhumation (burial), in megalithic tombs (tombs constructed out of large slabs of stone). These burial places were traditionally arranged to face the east, and were covered with trapezoidal long cairns.

The Use of Long Cairns

Long cairns came in a variety of formats, but in Ireland the most widespread example was the court cairn. Typically, Neolithic people constructed this with an elongated trapezoid or double trapezoidal outline, edged with rows of orthostats (vertical stone slabs) or a drystone wall. The axis of the cairn ran east–west, and at the entrance to the tomb was a semicircular forecourt. This area was sometimes paved and probably held a ritual significance, since precious objects were frequently interred here. On rare occasions, long cairns were built with courts at both ends. The forecourt is thought to have been designed as a gathering place for the mourners, at the time of the burial. A standard example could easily have accommodated around fifty people.

The internal arrangement of the cairn varied considerably. The simplest examples featured one or two chambers, separated by a combination of sills and jambs. More complex variants also had side-chambers, often classified as transepted gallery graves. Court cairns were limited almost exclusively to the north of Ireland and south-western Scotland, and this has given rise to their alternate name:

'Clyde–Carlingford tombs'. In Ireland itself, more than 300 have been located north of a line between Dundalk and Westport, while a mere half-dozen have been discovered in the south. The tombs appear to have remained in use for a considerable period, judging by the variety of pottery finds within them. Estimated dates range from 3500 BC to the end of the Neolithic period in 2200 BC.

Signs of human habitation are far less easy to come by, principally because structures were made of wood and other perishable materials. Some of the best-preserved finds have been made underneath long cairns, protected by the burial places above them, but the most famous site is at Lough Gur. The area surrounding this tiny lake in County Limerick was excavated extensively in the 1930s and 1940s, revealing no fewer than sixteen settlements from the Neolithic or Neolithic/Bronze Age periods. Surviving traces of the original ground-plans indicate that the houses were either circular or rectangular, and were centred around a hearth. In the rectangular huts, postholes suggest that the home was divided into three sections. The central area with the hearth was used for daytime activities, while the side-aisles were reserved for storage and sleeping. It is uncertain what material was used for the walls, although mud and turf are the most likely candidates.

Links with the Beaker Folk?

Lough Gur is also notable for the sheer volume of its pottery finds, with one site alone yielding more than 11,000 sherds. Most of these items were pieces of Lough Gur ware, but examples of Beaker ware were also unearthed. At the time of the excavations, this type of pottery was very uncommon in Ireland, although many similar discoveries have since come to light. This has raised the question of whether there was a sizeable migration of Beaker Folk into Ireland, during the transition from the Neolithic era to the Bronze Age.

Beaker culture extended over much of continental Europe, where it was principally linked with an aristocratic caste of warrior-archers. It takes its name from the highly decorative style of their pottery, which frequently displayed combed, grooved or corded decoration, although the so-called 'Beaker package' also included martial artefacts, such as tanged daggers, barbed arrowheads and stone bracers. More importantly, perhaps, the

Beaker Folk appear to have been the first to make widespread use of copper. Their use of this metal has encouraged the idea that Beaker Folk travelled to Ireland to exploit that region's plentiful natural ores. However, Beaker products were widely distributed throughout the continent, and it is also possible that Irish examples were simply acquired through trading contacts.

The Building of Passage-Graves

By contrast, there was certainly an important influx of new settlers c. 2500 BC, when the builders of the monumental passage-graves made their initial appearance on Irish soil. They arrived from Brittany, constructing their first overseas tombs on Anglesey and the Welsh coast, before moving across the sea to Ireland. The burial practices of these extraordinary tomb-builders differed considerably from those of earlier peoples. First, they preferred to place their dead in cemeteries, rather than in individual tombs. In most cases, these consisted of a single, monumental passage-grave, surrounded by a cluster of smaller graves. Often, this principal tomb would be located some distance from its satellite tombs, a typical example being Maeve's Cairn or Lump at Knocknarea, which adjoins the cemetery of Carrowmore, County Sligo.

Second, the new tomb-builders displayed a preference for locating their monuments above ground and on lofty sites which dominated the surrounding countryside. The graves themselves were essentially chamber tombs, approached, as the name suggests, through a narrow entrance passage. The main chamber was usually constructed out of orthostats topped by lintels, although the more impressive examples featured a corbelled roof. Using this technique – which involved placing layers of overlapping stones in ever-diminishing circles and then topping them with a capstone – builders were able to give their vaults extra height. The finished chamber was then

MAEVE'S LUMP, KNOCKNAREA, COUNTY SLIGO
In popular lore this prehistoric cairn is thought to be the burial place of Maeve, a mythical queen of Connacht and a goddess of sovereignty.

covered with a mound. Three recesses, at the sides and far end of the chamber, gave it a cruciform shape.

Cremation was more common than inhumation, and the remains of the deceased were often accompanied by elaborate grave-goods, including personal ornaments, decorated Carrowkeel pottery and ritual stone balls. The most common types of jewellery to be interred were poppy- or mushroom-headed antler pins, and beads or pendants made out of semi-precious stones. Carrowkeel vessels are thought to have been used for carrying the ashes into the grave, although it is also possible that they contained offerings of food. Weapons and tools were usually excluded from the most sacred areas of the tomb.

More than 300 passage-graves have been identified in Ireland, but the most celebrated examples occur in a corridor that stretches from the Drogheda coastline to County Sligo in the north-west. They include the cemeteries of Carrowmore, Carrowkeel, Loughcrew and the great monuments in the Boyne Valley, in County Meath.

The Monuments of the Boyne Valley

The Boyne complex was dominated by three massive tumuli – Newgrange, Knowth and Dowth – although the site also included a series of smaller satellite tombs, several standing stones and a few earthen enclosures. In early Irish legend, the place was known as *Brug na Bóinne* (Palace of the Boyne) and was deemed to have been the abode of ancient gods (see p.18). In terms of both its scale and its grandeur, this association is easy to comprehend.

The easternmost member of the trio is Dowth, which is 85 metres (280 feet) in diameter and 16 metres (50 feet) high. It suffered badly during early excavations (1847–8) and was described by one official as the 'flea market' of Irish passage-graves. Nevertheless, its size is impressive and it contains three orthostats with chevron, spiral and lozenge designs. The mound itself covers two graves that are set side-by-side in the western half of the tomb. One of these features a circular chamber with a corbelled roof.

KNOWTH, COUNTY MEATH
This is the entrance to one of the satellite graves in the Boyne complex, Ireland's most important group of megalithic monuments.

Knowth also has two passage-graves and, once again, one of these has corbel vaulting. In this instance, however, the graves were constructed back-to-back, with the two funerary chambers at the centre. The western example, with its distinctive 'elbow' in the passage, is particularly close to Breton models. The mound is even larger than that at Dowth, and was built up from a variety of materials – shale, clay, turf and stone. It is surrounded by no fewer than eighteen satellite tombs of varying types. At least one of these (Site 16) predated the main tumulus, since the outline of Knowth's enclosure was altered to accommodate the smaller tomb. The internal decoration of the two passage-graves is more elaborate than at Dowth. Orthostats in the western tomb are adorned with boxed rectangles and a stylized human face, while the eastern grave contains an elaborate stone basin covered in abstract, geometric designs, which was used as a receptacle for cremated remains.

Knowth continued to fascinate the generations that followed its construction. During the early historical period it was adapted for domestic habitation and new souterrains (underground chambers) were constructed within the mound. Later, during the Christian era, it was occupied by the kings of northern Brega (an extensive plain between the Rivers Boyne and Liffey) and, in the twelfth century, it was claimed by Richard de Flemming, a Hiberno-Norman baron.

One of the most controversial aspects of Knowth is the orientation of the two tombs, which face directly east and west. This has encouraged speculation that their builders deliberately sited them to correspond with the rising of the sun at the spring and autumn equinoxes. By and large, this kind of arrangement is less common in the passage-graves than in other Irish megalithic tombs. Nevertheless, the monuments on the Boyne appear to have been an exception. This is particularly noticeable at the Newgrange tumulus, which was undoubtedly aligned with the winter solstice in mind. On 21 December the first rays of the rising sun pass through a 'roof-box', situated above the entrance to the tomb, then shine down the full length of the passage and the burial chamber, reaching as far as the stone basin on the end recess.

FOLLOWING PAGE – LOUGHCREW, COUNTY MEATH
At Loughcrew, otherwise known as the 'Hill of the Witch',
there are around thirty chambered cairns and passage-graves.
Many of the stones have been decorated with geometrical designs.

> *Thus it was that Oenghus stole the palace of Newgrange from his father. At the festival of Samhain, the time of changes, he went to the Dagda and begged him to grant him the tenancy of the* Brug na Bóinne *for the space of a night and a day. The Dagda gazed fondly on his son and readily agreed to yield up his palace on those terms. He departed immediately and, for the space of a night and a day, Oenghus held the kingship of the fairy mound.*
>
> *At the end of the allotted time, the Dagda came again to* Brug na Bóinne *and requested the return of his palace. But Oenghus refused his father, explaining that he was now the rightful owner of the mound. He had been granted lordship over it for a night and a day and, since the passage of time consists of nothing more than night and day, following each other in endless succession, he was now master of the palace for all eternity. Then the Dagda realized that he had been tricked. He went away, taking his household and his people with him, leaving Oenghus to enjoy Goibhniu's ale and the feast that never failed.*

The Taking of the Fairy Mound
from the Mythological Cycle

Newgrange – Resting Place of the High Kings

The most celebrated of all Irish tombs, and the focus of many ancient legends, is Newgrange. Both the Dagda, the father of the gods, and Oenghus, the god of love, were said to have resided there (see p.16), and it was also the fabled resting place of the high kings of Tara. The huge, kidney-shaped mound was discovered by accident in 1699, when labourers were constructing a nearby road. Inside, there appears to be only a single passage-grave, although many archaeologists believe that a second tomb remains to be discovered. Even so, the existing chamber is highly impressive. It has a cruciform design and a remarkable hexagonal vault, composed of corbelled stones that weigh as much as a tonne apiece.

The most outstanding feature of Newgrange is its carved decoration. The massive kerbstone (entrance stone) features a sinuous blend of spiral and lozenge motifs; a variation of these, combined with cupmarks and axe symbols, can also be found on Stone K52, a kerbstone at the opposite side of the tumulus. Inside, other slabs were also decorated by the people who constructed the tombs. The best-known example, at the end of the passage, features a perfectly formed triple spiral; elsewhere there are lozenges, zigzags and concentric arcs.

Inevitably, frequent attempts have been made to interpret the meaning of the assorted decoration on Irish passage-graves. Many of these have taken their cue from the megalithic tombs of Brittany, which served as models for the Irish monuments. Particular attention has been focused on the passage-grave of Gavr'inis ('Island of

A RACE OF GIANTS

The Celts regarded Ireland's megalithic monuments with a transparent sense of awe. Not surprisingly, perhaps, they felt that these magnificent structures could only have been produced by gods or superhuman heroes. As a result, the most striking tombs figured prominently in early legends. Thus, Newgrange was known as the home of Oenghus, the god of love, while the high king Cormac mac Airt (see p.88) held court at Tara, surrounded by Finn and the Fianna, his brotherhood of warriors. At the Neolithic cemetery of Carrowmore the principal cairn was named after Maeve, the evil queen of Connacht who proved such an implacable enemy of Cú Chulainn (see p.31). In a broader, mythical context, she was also a goddess of war, sovereignty and sexual power, which made her a worthy owner of the lofty site. Surrounding Maeve's Cairn, the tombs at Carrowmore were popularly known as the burial mounds of the Fir Bolg, a shadowy race of invaders who are said to have taken control of Ireland in prehistoric times.

In some versions of Irish legends, the ancient gods and heroes were perceived as giants. This encouraged the belief that some of the early tombs were nothing more than items of furniture belonging to Irish deities. Many portal tombs, for example, became known as the beds of Diarmaid and Gráinne – a pair of runaway lovers who travelled through the countryside, sleeping in the open air. Similarly, the Giant's Causeway was thought to be part of a bridge constructed by Finn, linking northern Ireland with Fingal's Cave on the island of Staffa (Fingal being the Scottish form of Finn).

NEWGRANGE, COUNTY MEATH (LEFT)
This massive kerbstone lies at the entrance to Newgrange. The spiral and lozenge designs inspired later generations of Celtic artists.

PROLEEK DOLMEN, COUNTY LOUTH (RIGHT)
Situated a few kilometres outside Dundalk, this remarkable balancing act is also known as the Giant's Load.

BRONZE CREMATION VESSEL

*Discovered at a hill-fort at Fore, County Meath, this fine
vessel was probably an import from Britain. Originally it had
a pair of bird's-head handles, but one of these is now lost.*

Goats'), the largest of the Breton tombs and the one that
is closest in spirit to Newgrange. Some of its motifs are
quite different – the female guardian spirits and the serpents – but one slab features three small hollows set into
a cartouche, an image that is directly comparable with
the cupmarks on a stone at Newgrange. More significantly still, Gavr'inis is the only Breton tomb that contains
profuse spiral decoration, and it can hardly be a coincidence that, like Newgrange, its passage was aligned by its
builders to receive the first rays of the midwinter sun.
This reinforces the widely held belief that the spiral motif
is meant to represent the motion of the sun.

The great unanswered mystery about the Boyne complex is why three great tumuli came to be built so close
together. A few authorities have speculated fancifully about
some long-forgotten dynasty, some line of Irish 'pharaohs'
who erected the tombs as memorials to their power. More
realistically, it has been seen as a sacred site, where people
who lived in the flimsiest and most incommodious of shel-
ters laboured long and hard to construct a fitting tribute to
the life-giving qualities of the sun. In purely artistic terms,
the decoration of Newgrange and its companions must also
have provided inspiration for the Celtic craftsmen who
were to arrive in the area many centuries later.

Portal and Wedge Tombs

While the passage-graves are probably the best-known
type of megalithic tomb in Ireland, other forms can also
be found. Portal tombs or dolmens (deriving from the
Breton words for 'stone' and 'table') were commonplace
in both the north and the south-east. The basic structure
is a single burial chamber, located above ground. A series
of upright slabs – sometimes as few as three – supports a
large capstone, which slants downwards from front to
back. Most chambers also become narrower at the rear
and are fronted by a pair of portal stones.

The obvious affinities between these chambers and the
court cairn have suggested that the portal dolmen is a
degenerate form of the latter. This remains unproved,
however, particularly as some portal tombs have

produced very ancient radiocarbon readings (as early as
c. 3290 BC for Grave 7 in Carrowmore cemetery). Within
the tombs, most burials seem to have taken the form of
cremation and the chambers are usually aligned towards
the east. A high proportion of the portal tombs are
concentrated in coastal areas or river valleys, perhaps
indicating that their architectural influence came from
overseas. The most striking examples of Irish dolmens
can be found at Kilclooney, in County Donegal, and at
Poulnabrone in the Burren. In later years the distinctive
shape of dolmens inspired many fanciful associations.
Often they were regarded as the remains of an ancient
race of Irish giants. In this context they were seen as beds,
tables or even quoits. Alternatively they were interpreted
as huge sacrificial altars, where druid priests carried

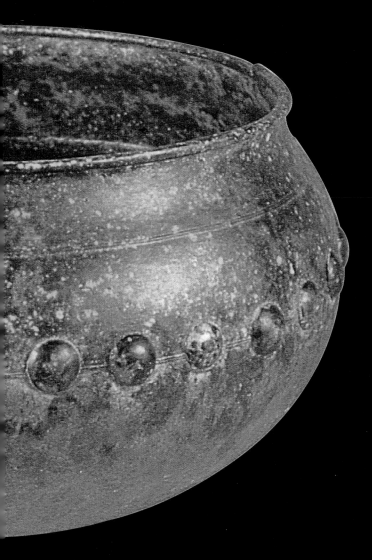

Single-Grave Burials

The megalithic tombs may have attracted most attention from archaeologists, but throughout the Late Neolithic/ Beaker period a much simpler burial procedure was also in operation. This involved single-grave burials in cists. In essence, a cist was a stone chest (the two words come from the same root), covered with side-slabs, a capstone and a small cairn. Burial places of this kind are sometimes known collectively as Linkardstown cists, after the extensively excavated site in County Carlow. Cists generally contained the remains of one or two adult males, sometimes placed in a crouched position and very often with disarticulated limbs. In addition, the grave usually contained round-bottomed hanging vessels. Styles varied, but much of the pottery was decorated Western Neolithic ware, featuring grooved or geometric designs.

Single-grave burials in cists became the norm during the Bronze Age, although the shape of the cists gradually became more varied, with elongated or polygonal cists offering an alternative to the traditional short chest. The dead were also frequently interred in pits or barrows. Within pits, the body might be contained in an urn, and the pit itself was sometimes covered with a slab. Barrows came in numerous shapes and sizes but generally consisted of low, rounded mounds and an encircling ditch. In most of these burials, the deceased – and it was only men who were buried in this way – was accompanied by a single vessel, placed closed to his head. Not surprisingly, these pots were thought to contain offerings of meat or drink, and were grouped together under the general heading of Food Vessel. Gradually, however, they were used to hold the cremated remains of the dead. In spite of its name, Food Vessel pottery is therefore essentially funerary ware.

If Bronze Age tombs are something of an anticlimax after the splendours of the Neolithic era, compensation comes in the emerging metalworking skills of native craftsmen. Nobody knows precisely how these developed in Ireland and the old theory that they were introduced by the Beaker Folk is being treated with ever greater caution. It seems more likely that the transition from stone to metal was a very gradual one, fostered by the region's increasing links with the outside world. In the course of time, these growing contacts would attract a new influx of settlers to Irish shores – the Celts.

out their grisly rites. In reality, of course, the dolmens predated the emergence of the druids.

The most prolific of the megalithic formats was the wedge tomb, which can be found in most parts of Ireland. Opinion is divided as to whether this derived from the *allées couvertes* (gallery-graves) of Brittany or was an indigenous development. Either way, the burial chamber generally assumes the form of a gallery with a wedge- or horseshoe-shaped layout. This is entered through a 'portico' or ante-chamber, flanked by a pair of portal stones and separated from the main burial area by a stone sill or jamb. The gallery may also be encircled by an outer wall and topped with a cairn. In spite of their abundance, relatively few wedge tombs have been excavated and knowledge of their development is thus quite sketchy.

CHAPTER TWO

THE ARRIVAL OF THE CELTS

The Celts had already been flourishing
for half a millennium when they became
the dominant force on Irish soil. By this
stage Celtic craftsmen had already honed
their designs to a peak of perfection,
particularly in the field of metalwork.
During the Iron Age these styles finally
began to circulate in Ireland, where they
would soon usher in a new tradition.

BLASKET ISLANDS, COUNTY KERRY
*Lying off the tip of the Dingle peninsula,
the islands house the remains of an anchoritic settlement,
dedicated to Brendan the Navigator.*

THE ARRIVAL OF THE CELTS

T[HE EARLY HISTORY] of Ireland is so closely bound up with the Celts that it is easy to gain the impression this is where they developed their inimitable style and culture. The Celts did not, however, originate in Ireland. They made their first appearance at the other end of Europe, at the start of the Iron Age. From around the sixth century BC, classical authors began referring to a race of people named the *Keltoi*, who had already spread across much of Europe. The Greek historian Hecataeus of Miletus (c. 550–476 BC) wrote an account of his travels in the West, in which he cited Narbonne and Marseilles as being settlements in or near a Celtic region. Similarly, the Greek historian Herodotus (c. 490–c. 425 BC) mentioned that the Celts were living beyond the Pillars of Hercules (the two promontories now known as the Rock of Gibraltar and Mount Acho at the tip of North Africa) and were one of the most westerly peoples in Europe.

From a classical viewpoint, the Celts were undoubtedly viewed as barbarians. The Greek historian Ephorus of Cyme (fourth century BC) described them as one of the four great barbarian races of the known world, together with the Libyans, the Persians and the Scythians. They consisted of a series of warlike tribes which numbered – among others – the Gauls, the Galatians and the Belgae. These tribes had no political centre and did not base their power within any strict territorial limits, but they were united by a number of social and cultural traits, which gave them sufficient cohesion to mount a genuine threat to their rivals. At the height of their power, the Celts even proved mighty enough to capture the strongholds of Rome (386 BC) and Delphi (279 BC).

Celtic Style

The factors that united the Celts included religion, dress, customs, language, social organization and military methods. These were first noticed in the central and eastern regions of Europe, but gradually spread to most parts of the continent. Ireland was one of the last areas to receive these influences, but it retained them the longest. In part, this was due to the rise of the Roman Empire, which overcame the military might of the Celts and suppressed many aspects of their culture. Ireland being one of the few places in Europe that did not come under the direct control of the Empire, it therefore became a haven for the purest forms of Celtic civilization.

The Celts flourished for hundreds of years and, during this time, their art and civilization inevitably fragmented

into a whole host of local variations. To maintain some kind of overview, archaeologists have traced their development through the changing styles of the artefacts discovered at two representative sites, Hallstatt and La Tène.

The Hallstatt site is a vast cemetery, containing approximately 3,000 graves. It is located in the Salzkammergut area of Upper Austria, about 50 kilometres (30 miles) to the east of Salzburg. The cemetery served the needs of local communities of salt-miners, who worked in the region for several centuries. Because of the length of their occupation and the remarkable preservative qualities of the salt in the soil, Hallstatt has yielded an astonishing range of finds. These include a drinking service and various weapons from a chieftain's tomb, which also contained a lavish scabbard decorated with stylized, figurative images that have been classified as early prototypes of Celtic design.

The site at La Tène was very different. Situated in Switzerland, on the northern reaches of Lake Neuchâtel, its purpose has prompted a variety of different interpretations. Some authorities believe that it was either an arsenal or a trading centre, but the most popular view is that it was a sacred place – an outdoor temple where precious objects were deposited as votive offerings. The majority of

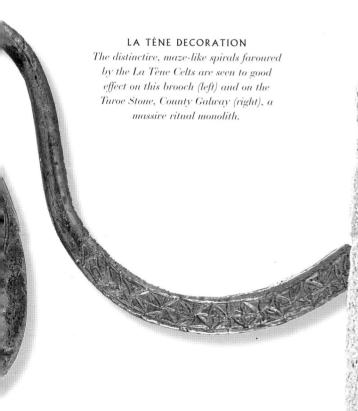

LA TÈNE DECORATION
The distinctive, maze-like spirals favoured by the La Tène Celts are seen to good effect on this brooch (left) and on the Turoe Stone, County Galway (right), a massive ritual monolith.

THE SHANNON ERNE WATERWAY
Watery sites were sacred to the Celts.
In ancient lore the River Shannon came
under the protection of Sinann,
granddaughter of the sea-god, Lir.

the sacrifices appear to have consisted of swords or spears, although some jewellery has also been found.

La Tène culture forms the second stage of the European Iron Age and covers a very broad period, lasting from approximately the fifth to the first centuries BC. It encompasses most of the major developments in Celtic civilization, from the Early Style – this fused elements from the classical world (mainly Greece and Etruria in central Italy), so-called 'Oriental' motifs from the Near East, and the geometric patterns popularized during the Hallstatt era in Europe into a single, distinctive style – to the Waldalgesheim phase or Vegetal Style. This period coincided with the great expansion of the Celts right across the continent, when their art forms reached full maturity and their culture was disseminated over the widest possible area. Stylized figurative designs still predominated, but craftsmen also displayed a great fondness for creating patterns from interweaving trails of foliage, thus giving the period its alternative name.

From around 290 BC a new trend became apparent. During the phase known as the Plastic Style, a greater appreciation of volume can be detected in Celtic artefacts. Designs became asymmetrical and three-dimensional, often involving playful distortions of animal and human

LA TÈNE SWORD
Fine weaponry was often deposited
in rivers, lakes or marshes, as a
form of sacrifice. This sword was
retrieved from the River Shannon,
in County Clare.

THE DOWRIS HOARD AND THE 'GREAT CLARE FIND'

The Irish period that is roughly equivalent to the Hallstatt culture is known as the Dowris phase (traditionally dated as c. 800–400 BC). This takes its name from a remarkable hoard, which was uncovered in 1825 by some potato-diggers at Whigsborough (previously Dowris), in County Offaly. The find included an extraordinary collection of axes, buckets, trumpets and crotals (musical instruments). These were made of bronze, but other discoveries from the Dowris period were fashioned out of gold. The most spectacular has entered folk myth as the 'Great Clare Find'.

In 1854 a group of construction workers were preparing land for the West Clare railway at Mooghaun North. One of them disturbed an ancient mound of stones, revealing a large hoard of glittering objects. There was a mad scramble, as the labourers rushed to grab their share of the treasure. Most of the items were sold off quickly, before any questions could be asked, but contemporary reports suggest that there were more than 130 golden bracelets, eight neck-rings or torcs, and a variety of smaller objects. The majority have long since disappeared, but around twenty-five have survived and can be seen in the National Museum of Ireland, in Dublin, and in the British Museum, London.

The Clare find was not, however, an isolated phenomenon. A considerable number of gold artefacts can be dated to the Irish Bronze Age and, since the metal was presumably imported, experts have interpreted this as evidence that there must have been well-established lines of contact between Ireland and continental Europe. The relative wealth of metalworking traditions in Ireland during the Dowris phase also boded well for La Tène influence there, for this culture was to be known, above all else, for the supreme quality of its metalwork.

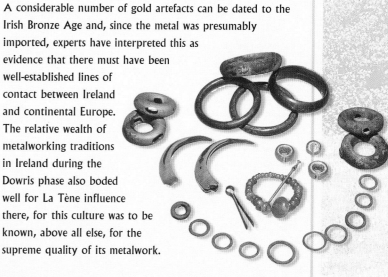

forms. This in turn was succeeded by the Hungarian Sword Style that takes its name from a new type of design found on Celtic weaponry. The decoration was flat and linear, marking a return to the spirit of the Early Style.

Inevitably, despite this rough framework for the development of Celtic influences, there was considerable local variation. The standard chronology is based on activity in the Celtic heartlands – Germany, Switzerland and central Europe – and can serve only as a guideline. Ireland, as one of the last outposts of Celtic influence, tended to reflect new styles at a later date than other parts of Europe. For archaeologists, there is also the thorny problem of deciding which artefacts were imported into Ireland and which were made there by native craftsmen.

The Origins of the Irish Celts?

In the past it was assumed that, at some point during the Iron Age, there was a large-scale migration of Celtic people into Ireland. This idea is now treated with considerable suspicion. Instead, it is more likely that the earliest Celtic influences came from overseas trading contacts, rather than from settlement (the timing and the route of which are both open to question). Some people believe that La Tène culture was introduced into northern Ireland from south-west Scotland and the north of England. Others suggest that it came directly from France and Spain, citing – in addition to archaeological evidence from the south of Ireland – the *Book of Invasions* (*Leabhar Gabhála*), an early but largely mythical account of Ireland's origins which described a race of invaders called the Milesians. These have sometimes been regarded as Iberians, largely on account of their heroic leader, Mil Espáine ('Soldier of Spain').

The archaeological evidence is inconclusive. Some traces of iron-working in Ireland may date back as far as the seventh century BC, and two sites in particular – Navan Fort in County Armagh and Rathtinaun in County Sligo – have produced iron fragments in a Late Bronze Age context. However, iron did not become the primary metal until around the third century BC. Similarly, around forty Hallstatt C swords and chapes (scabbard

STANDING STONE, DUNMORE HEAD, COUNTY KERRY
This monolith has an ogham inscription along its edge.
The purpose of these inscribed stones is uncertain, but they
may have been territorial markers or memorials to the dead.

GOIDEL GLAS

Goidel Glas ('Green Goidel') was hailed by the Celts as the inventor of the Gaelic language. His legend is recounted in the pseudo-historical Book of Invasions, together with details of the Gaels themselves. According to this source, Goidel's origins were extremely exotic: his father was Niúl, an ancestor of the Milesians, who was said to have given his name to the River Nile; his mother was Scota, a daughter of the Pharaoh Cingris. In his youth, Goidel was almost killed after being bitten by a snake, but Moses managed to heal him with a touch of his rod. Even so, the wound left him with a green scar, which was the cause of his nickname. Moses then went on to prophesy that Goidel would live in a land that was free of snakes – a clear reference to the coming of St Patrick, who would rid Ireland of its paganism (symbolized by serpents). Goidel devised Gaelic out of the various languages that he learned from his grandfather Fénius Farsaid ('Fénius the Pharisee'), who had been present at the Tower of Babel, where the builders worked in seventy-two different languages.

attachments) have been discovered at a variety of Irish sites, most with long blades and a distinctive 'eared' handle, where the terminal is forked. The finest example has been retrieved from the River Shannon near Killaloe, County Clare, where it was probably deposited as a sacrifice. It dates back to c. 600 BC but, in common with others of its kind, is a bronze copy of an iron Hallstatt weapon. In the remaining cases it is impossible to gauge whether the weapon was made by native craftsmen or was simply an import.

A Question of Language

However it arrived on the island, the Irish version of Celtic culture differed from its European counterparts in at least one vital respect, its language. The Celts communicated in an Indo-European tongue, which first developed in the region between the Black Sea and the Baltic. In its earliest stages this language was defined as 'Common Celtic', but it soon evolved three major dialects: Gaulish, Brythonic and Gaelic or Goidelic. As the name

implies, Gaulish was the language of the Gauls (the peoples living in modern France, Belgium, Luxemburg, south-west Germany and northern Italy). It gradually disappeared when those people came under the yoke of Roman rule. Brythonic provided the basis for Breton, Welsh and Cornish, the first two of which are still widely spoken in their native regions. Gaelic, meanwhile, developed into Irish, Scots Gaelic and Manx.

The principal difference between the Brythonic and Gaelic dialects concerned a major consonant change,

which is thought to have occurred in the first millennium BC. At this stage, the original Indo-European 'qu' was replaced with a 'p' in some areas. The Brythonic form became what is termed a P-Celtic language; the Goidels retained the Q-Celtic tongue. The Goidels, incidentally, took their name from Goidel Glas (see p.28), a legendary hero described in the *Book of Invasions*. He was said to have invented the Irish language in biblical times, by combining elements from the seventy-two different languages that were in use at the Tower of Babel.

For religious reasons, the Irish Celts did not allow their learning or records to be set down in writing, so there is no concrete evidence relating to the early development of the Irish language. The first examples were actually preserved in ogham – a very basic form of writing, in which the alphabet was conveyed through a series of straight or slanting lines, notched on to pieces of stone. Despite its obvious limitations, ogham appears to have carried some ritual significance and was mainly reserved for memorial inscriptions.

Paradoxically, the absence of a written language has proved beneficial for historians, since it encouraged the Celts to develop an elaborate and highly efficient system of oral transmission. Through this means a large body of vernacular literature and law tracts was preserved for many centuries, before finally being written down. The oldest surviving manuscripts date only from the medieval period but, by comparing these with accounts of the continental Celts made by classical authors, it seems safe to assume that they may reflect conditions in Ireland during the Iron Age.

The Brehon Laws

The legal tracts that have come down to us are known as the Brehon Laws, taking their name from the Celtic word for a judge. According to tradition, these laws were codified in the fifth century, on the specific orders of St Patrick, but had been amassed over the course of many centuries. They covered two main areas: the *Senchas Már* (Great Tradition), which dealt with civil law, and the Book of Acaill, which referred to criminal matters. It was the duty of the *brehon* (a hereditary post) to preserve these texts, rather than actually to dispense justice, so he might best be described as a legal authority.

The Brehon Laws were a compilation of legal records, rather than a series of statutes. Their greatest importance lies in the fact that they predate Roman law, making them the oldest codified legal system in Europe. Significantly, too, there are some close affinities with Hindu law, which points to a common source in Indo-European custom. A typical example concerns the use of fasting. In cases of debt, where one or both parties enjoyed exalted status (*nemed*), it was normal practice for the plaintiff to sit outside the defendant's house and fast from sunset to sunrise. This made the latter honour-bound to submit the

THE BOOK OF INVASIONS

The *Leabhar Gabhála*, or Book of Invasions, is one of the richest sources of information about Ireland in the prehistoric period. The oldest surviving version of the text can be found in the twelfth-century Book of Leinster, though various sections of the narrative were clearly composed many centuries earlier. The compilers' aim was to produce an anthology of the myths and pseudo-historical tales about Ireland's origins, correlating these with events in the Bible. The result, according to one modern commentator, was a 'masterpiece of muddled medieval miscellany'.

The text specifies seven distinct invasions of Ireland in prehistoric times and, although several of these are clearly inventions, scholars have speculated extensively about the remainder. The first 'invaders' were cited as Cesair, granddaughter of Noah, together with her followers; the Partholonians, an eastern Mediterranean race; and the Nemedians, who have sometimes been identified with the Erainn, a genuine P-Celtic people. The Nemedians did battle with the Fomorians, the legendary race of demonic pirates, whose evil deeds were probably coloured by medieval memories of Viking raids. They in turn were succeeded by the Fir Bolg, who were said to have introduced iron weapons into the country. Attempts have been made to link them to a number of historical tribes, including the Erainn, the Domnann (P-Celts from Britain), the Galióin (the founders of Leinster) and the Belgae. The final two groups of invaders were the Tuatha Dé Danaan (the ancient gods of Ireland) and the Milesians, who have often been seen as fictionalized versions of the Goidels or Gaels.

case to arbitration. If he ignored the fast, he lost the privileges of his rank and could be treated like a commoner. As the text states:

He who does not give a pledge to fasting is an evader of all. He who disregards all things is paid by neither god nor man.

This process has many similarities with the Hindu system of *dharna*.

The early Irish laws shed light on a whole gamut of topics, ranging from bee-keeping to water-rights. One of the most ancient tracts was known as 'The Judgments of Dian Cécht', and dealt with provision for the sick and injured. If a man wounded another member of the community, he was obliged to take him into his household and supervise his convalescence. In addition to feeding the victim, this might involve financial support for his family or retinue and even supplying a substitute to carry out his work. The treatise was named after Dian Cécht, the physician of the Celtic gods. According to tradition, he presided over a healing spring that could resuscitate any warrior, apart from those who had been decapitated.

The Ulster Cycle

While the Brehon Laws have mainly attracted the attention of specialists, early Irish legends and sagas have exerted a much broader and more popular appeal. Their mythical subject matter covers a broad range of themes, including pseudo-historical accounts of ancient invasions and the reigns of imaginary kings; poetic travelogues of the Irish countryside; and colourful tales explaining how individual places acquired their names. The core of this early literature, however, is the Ulster Cycle, which revolves around the exploits of Cú Chulainn, who is partly a god and partly a superhuman warrior hero. In the *Táin Bó Cuailgne* (The Cattle Raid of Cooley) – the central story in the cycle – he battles single-handedly to protect the people of Ulster from the invading armies of Connacht. Under the leadership of Maeve (another euhemerized figure, who is part goddess and part evil warrior-queen) the armies of Connacht have come in search of a magical bull, exploiting the fact that the men of Ulster are disabled by a curse. Cú Chulainn denies them their prize, however, forcing them to flee back to their own territory, before meeting his death through the treachery of Maeve.

As with the Brehon Laws, the text of the Ulster Cycle survives only in a series of comparatively late manuscripts. The principal sources are the Book of the Dun Cow (*Leabhar na h-Uidhre*), the Book of Leinster (*Leabhar Laighneach*) and the Yellow Book of Lecan (*Leabhar Buide Lecáin*). The first of these was transcribed at the monastery of Clonmacnoise, in County Offaly, in c. 1100, where it was treated with the reverence of a holy relic, because a local legend claimed that the vellum manuscript was written on the hide of a pet cow that had once belonged to St Ciaran (c. 512–c. 45). The Book of Leinster was compiled by Finn Mac Gorman, a bishop of Kildare, in c. 1160 and, in common with the other manuscripts, contains an assortment of material. In addition to the *Táin*, it features the Book of Invasions and the *Dinnshenchas*, the primary source for topographical lore. The Yellow Book of Lecan was produced considerably later than the other two (c. 1390), but features the most ancient version of the Ulster Cycle.

Although these manuscripts were products of the Middle Ages, the action of the *Táin* belongs to a much earlier society. Estimates vary dramatically, but most authorities assign it to a period between the second century BC and the fourth century AD. As such, it provides invaluable insights into the social organization and values of Iron Age Ireland.

KNOCKNAREA, COUNTY SLIGO
An aerial view of Maeve's Cairn or Lump.
A local tradition ascribes its construction to
Eógan Bél, the last pagan king of Connacht.

Celtic Society

For all the looseness of their political links, the internal structure of Celtic communities appears to have been firmly regulated. The basic unit was the *tuath* (the tribe or clan) and, by extension, the territory that it inhabited. In general, a typical *tuath* would have been able to provide a force of anything between 500 and 3,000 men. Larger units were described as a *trícha cét* ('thirty hundreds'), which indicated that its army numbered at least 3,000 warriors.

Each *tuath* was governed by a chieftain or king (*rí*). Initially, this was undoubtedly a sacred office, the king being deemed to have divine ancestry and his inauguration involving a ritual marriage with a goddess of sovereignty. Maeve, Cú Chulainn's adversary, was one of a number of deities who could fulfil this role. The practice inspired a number of Irish tales about hideous crones, who were suddenly transformed into radiant, supernatural beauties when they were embraced by a future king.

The people of the tuath owed their loyalty and obedience to the king, but the ruler in turn was also bound by certain obligations. In particular, it was believed that the fortunes of the chieftain and his land were closely intertwined. Both the character and the actions of the king had to be beyond reproach, or his subjects would suffer. In the legend of King Bres, for example, the countryside became infertile when the king neglected to observe the necessary laws of hospitality.

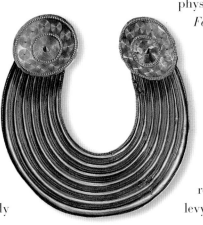

GOLD COLLAR
This sumptuous gorget dates from the Late Bronze Age and was discovered at Gleninsheen, County Clare. Neck decoration of this kind was unique to Ireland.

MOUND OF THE HOSTAGES, TARA, COUNTY MEATH
The hostages in question are said to have been taken by one of the earliest Irish kings, Niall Noígiallach (Niall of the Nine Hostages).

There were three levels of kingship, namely the *rí*, the *ruiri* ('superior king') and the *rí ruirech* ('king of superior kings'). The notion of an *ard rí* ('high king') was a later development. Below the king, the *tuath* was also divided into three main classes: the *flaithi* ('lords'), the *áes dána* ('men of art') and the *grád féne* (the land-tillers). The *flaithi* were essentially warriors, but the other two terms are slightly more complex. The 'men of art' comprised the entire professional classes. In addition to the poets – who often acted as royal advisers – it included physicians, lawyers and craftsmen. *Féne* or *Féni* was another name for the Goidels, the original Celtic settlers. As such, the word specified both a freeman and an inhabitant of the purest Irish stock; it is the source of 'Fenian', a term coined in the early nineteenth century. Most of the peasant class worked for the *flaithi*, binding themselves to a *célsine* or 'clientship'. In return for labouring on the land and a levy of food-rent (a tax paid with food), they were entitled to some grazing stock of their own.

Perhaps the most crucial element in early Celtic society was the strength of the family unit. Within each *tuath* this had far more importance than the rights of any particular individual. The traditional family group was the *derbfhine*, the 'family of four generations' (that is to say, the descendants of a common great-grandfather). Within this group, each male member held the same status. When questions of succession to land or a title arose, the matter was not automatically decided by age or direct lineage – a cousin or brother might easily take precedence over a first-born son if the *derbfhine* decided that this should be the case.

The close ties within both the *derbfhine* and the *tuath* were further strengthened by a number of important social customs. Chief among these was the Celtic system of fosterage. In early Irish society it was extremely common for children to be placed with foster-parents, even if their blood relatives were still alive. This might be done for a number of different reasons. Sometimes the motive was diplomatic, linking one family with a potentially useful neighbour; sometimes it was carried out in the hope of gaining advancement for the youngster, by placing him or her in a princely household; at other times it was the equivalent of a form of apprenticeship. In this context druids or *fili* (a type of poet or seer) and high-ranking craftsmen proved especially popular as foster-parents, since it was assumed that they would pass on their highly specialized skills to their young charges.

The implications of the fosterage system can be detected in both the Brehon Laws and the mythological tales. The former outline many of the routine details of the custom. They indicate, for example, the scale of fosterage fees that were paid. These ranged from three *séts* for the son of a peasant to thirty *séts* for the child of a royal household (two *séts* being roughly equivalent to the price of a milch cow). The legal tracts also specified the type of training that was to be given to the children, as well as the length of the fosterage period. In most cases

Cú Chulainn, the future hero of Ulster, has been born under miraculous circumstances. Immediately, his fellow countrymen rush to offer their services as foster-parents:

> *The news was swiftly passed to the men of Ulster. They were delighted to hear about the baby, and each man offered to raise the child and instruct him in his own special skills. As their arguments became very fierce, Conchobar decided that they should return to Emain to consult Morann, the judge… When they arrived there, Morann gave his judgment. "It is for Conchobar to raise the child, for he is next of kin to him. But let Sencha the poet instruct him in speech and oratory; let Fergus the warrior hold him on his knees; and let Amergin the sage be his tutor." And he added: "This child will be praised by all, by chariot drivers and soldiers, by kings and seers. He will avenge all your wrongs; he will defend your fords and fight all your battles."*

THE BIRTH OF CÚ CHULAINN
from the Ulster Cycle

this lasted from the age of seven until the youngster reached maturity (fourteen for a girl and seventeen for a boy). The laws also set out obligations that the children owed to their foster-parents, particularly when the latter reached old age or suffered from ill health.

In the heroic sagas the practical benefits of fosterage were vividly demonstrated. In the tales of the Ulster Cycle, for example, the fostering process created a special bond between warriors which far exceeded the normal bounds of military camaraderie. The climax of the *Táin*, for example, takes the form of a protracted duel between Cú Chulainn and Ferdia, one of his many foster-brothers. Both men are extremely reluctant to do battle with one another, and their epic encounter is conducted in a sombre, almost funereal atmosphere. In the intervals between the fighting, they tend each other's wounds and reminisce about the happiness of their shared boyhood, and Cú Chulainn's eventual victory is portrayed as a scene of high tragedy, rather than a memorable victory. This kind of tie must have been evident on genuine battlefields, for several classical authors noted the fierce, almost frenzied loyalty of Celtic warriors.

The expansive nature of the family unit was also affected by the Celtic system of marriage. Surviving law tracts make it clear that several different kinds of union were recognized, providing another link with Indian custom. No fewer than ten classes of wife were described in Irish records: some were permanent partners (the distinctions relating purely to the size of the marriage portion); other matches were clearly temporary. Any marriage could be ended by mutual agreement but, even without this, it was lawful for a man to take a second wife.

Detailed information about the relative rights of the principal wife and the concubine make it is easy to see how this situation could increase the need for a workable fosterage system. It also helps to explain an apparent inconsistency in many of the Celtic legends. Romantic tales were a favourite with early storytellers – Cú Chulainn's lengthy and arduous courtship of Emer, for

example, is one of the highlights of Irish literature. Yet, despite his protestations of undying love, the Ulster Cycle contains references to Cú Chulainn's numerous other liaisons, none of which provokes any censorious reaction from the storyteller.

Celtic Dwellings

The social structure of early Celtic life is reflected far more vividly in Ireland's literature than in its archaeological remains, which present difficulties both of dating and

CRAGGAUNOWEN PROJECT, COUNTY CLARE
This reconstruction of a crannog was the brainchild of the late John Hunt, who wanted to demonstrate how a prehistoric settlement might have looked.

FOLLOWING PAGE – NAVAN FORT, COUNTY ARMAGH
This is thought to be the site of Emain Macha, an ancient capital of Ulster.

of interpretation. Although a number of elaborate 'royal' sites have been identified, more humble abodes have yielded far less information.

The most common type of dwelling is thought to have been the protected farmstead. These came in different forms, but the oldest was probably the crannog – essentially an artificial island, built in a lake, bog or other watery site. In structures of this kind, the early Irish used the natural defences of the landscape to shield themselves from intruders. The simplest examples consisted of little more than mounds of brushwood or timber (*crann* is the Irish word for tree), but stones might also be used. The most elaborate structures were piled up well above the water level, enclosed within a circular palisade and had a causeway linking them to the shore. Crannogs of this kind were likely to have been the preserve of the wealthy, since the construction work would have required a considerable labour force. The crannog at Lagore, County Meath, for instance, was traditionally regarded as the home of the kings of South Brega.

Along with Lagore, the best-known examples of crannogs are found at Ballinderry, County Offaly, and

Rathtinaun in Lough Gara, County Sligo. The former was probably built during the Early Christian period and once featured an impressive palisade. Rathtinaun was one of around 300 crannogs that were exposed when Lough Gara was drained in the 1950s.

A Range of Ring-Forts

The other type of site that appears to date back to the Iron Age is the ring-fort. This term is used very broadly to denote a small homestead, ringed by a number of banks or ditches. The central enclosure normally contained one or more houses, together with a shelter for some livestock. Mention of the word 'fort' may prove confusing, since most of these structures were designed for

farmers and had no military overtones. Their purpose was as much to prevent the inhabitants' animals from straying as it was to keep outsiders at bay.

There are many different kinds of ring-fort. The simplest variety, in which the perimeter takes the form of one or more earthen ramparts, is usually known as a *rath*, but is sometimes also called a *lios*, although strictly speaking this refers only to the central enclosure. Where the outer ring is made of stone, the ring-fort is usually known as a *cathair* or *caiseal* (frequently anglicized as cashel). Evidently this was a more formidable dwelling than the *rath*, although a genuine stronghold was termed a *daingean* or *dun*.

As with crannogs, the origin and dating of ring-forts have been the subject of much debate. It has been suggested that they were first devised in Ireland, perhaps as a development from the Neolithic settlements typified by those at Lough Gur. Opinion has also been divided as to whether they first became common during the Iron Age or were primarily an Early Christian phenomenon. If nothing else, it does at least seem clear that ring-forts were introduced during the Iron Age, since a few isolated examples have been firmly dated within that period. These include the earthen raths at Cush, County Limerick; Lugg, County Dublin; Feewore, County Galway; and the celebrated *Ráth na Seanaid* (Rath of the Synods) at Tara, County Meath.

Tara – Seat of the High Kings?

The romantic associations of Tara have always overshadowed the precise nature of its archaeological remains. For centuries it was regarded as the seat of the high kings of Ireland and the focus of a number of important rituals; before that it was deemed to be the capital of the shadowy kingdom of Brega. In purely archaeological terms, however, it is a complex, multi-period site with around two dozen different features. Several of these are raths, among them the *Ráth na Ríogh* (Rath of the Kings), the *Ráth Gráinne* (named after the legendary heroine who eloped with Diarmaid) and the *Ráth Laoghaire*, which owes its title to the pagan high king who was confronted by St Patrick.

On the face of it, the Rath of the Synods has the least appropriate nickname of them all. It stems from an old legend that a number of Irish saints – among them, St

---

EMAIN MACHA

Emain Macha (now Navan Fort) was one of the most important sites of early Irish legend. It was the capital of Ulster, where Conchobar ruled in splendour during the epic tale of the Cattle Raid of Cooley. His fabulous palace, which was known as *Cráebruad* or 'Red Branch', boasted nine assembly rooms fashioned out of red yew and bronze, while his private chamber had a silver ceiling and pillars made of gold. Such was the fame of the place that the Ulster Cycle was once better known as the Red Branch Cycle.

There are several explanations of how Emain Macha received its name, but the most colourful revolves around a boastful lord named Crunniuc. At a royal fair, he bragged that his wife, Macha, could outrun the king's horses. Stung by his arrogance, the monarch ordered the race to take place, even though Macha was heavily pregnant. She duly won, but the exertion caused her to give birth to twins at the end of the course ('Emain Macha' may be translated as 'the twins of Macha'). Angered by her ordeal, Macha placed a curse on the men of Ulster, which would weaken them fatally during their coming conflict with Connacht. In reality Macha was a war goddess, although she has also been cited as the founder of Armagh (from *Ard Macha*, meaning the 'Heights of Macha').

Patrick, St Adamnán (c. 625–704) and St Ruadhán (sixth century) – held synods within the enclosure. Unfortunately, the sacred reputation of the place also attracted the attention of a group known as the British Israelites, who conducted an amateurish excavation of the site (1899–1902), in the hope of finding the Ark of the Covenant. In the process, the group caused considerable damage to the rath, while also failing to record their finds systematically. Nevertheless, a subsequent dig (1952–3) established that, at different periods, this rath had served as both a burial place and a habitation site. The grave mound contained the remains of both cremations and inhumations, while other parts of the enclosure included traces of a succession of wooden dwellings. Here, archaeologists discovered a number of Roman-style artefacts, including fragments of pottery, glass, a seal and a lock. These suggested that the site was at its most active between the first and third centuries AD.

According to tradition, the Rath of the Kings was built by the mythical Cormac mac Airt (his reign is dated in the Annals 227–66), supposedly the first of the high kings to take his seat at Tara. Two small, circular enclosures within the rath show the strength of this tradition. They are called the *Forradh* (Royal Seat) and *Teach Chormaic* (Cormac's House). Nevertheless, this area is clearly very much older than these names suggest. It contains the most ancient part of the entire Tara complex, a Neolithic passage-grave known by the evocative title *Dumha na nGiall* (Mound of the Hostages), and a pillar-stone called the *Lia Fáil* (Stone of Destiny), which seems to date from the Iron Age (see p.88).

Navan Fort – a Ritual Centre

The other great 'royal site' of this period is Navan Fort, in County Armagh. For many years this has been identified with Emain Macha, the capital of the Ulstermen, which features in the tales from the Ulster Cycle. Attempts have also been made to link it with Isamnion, one of the place-names featured on Ptolemy's map of Ireland (second century AD) and culled from an earlier source. In fact, neither of these associations is entirely consistent with the archaeological facts, which point to two main periods of activity. During the first of these, the site appears to have been used for domestic habitation; during the second, it became a major ritual centre.

A few scattered finds of fragments of pottery and flint confirm that the site had been occupied since Neolithic times, but the first main settlement was built by an Early Iron Age community, in the seventh century BC. Postholes and foundation trenches mark the site of a series of circular huts, and these can be linked with a varied selection of finds. Among other things, archaeologists unearthed some bronze tools (a socketed axe and sickle), a variety of pins and glass beads, a gaming die made out of bone, part of a winged chape from a Hallstatt C scabbard, and hundreds of tiny potsherds.

Undoubtedly, the most unusual discovery was the skull of a barbary ape, dating from around the third century BC. The reason for the animal's presence is unknown but, if nothing else, it demonstrates the remarkable extent of some overseas contacts during the prehistoric period.

Even at this early stage, Navan Fort was situated very close to a number of ritual sites. These included a pair of stone circles, now largely destroyed, and a man-made pool, known as 'the King's Stables', which is thought to date from the Late Bronze Age. Their ritual element may help to account for the dramatic shift in character that Navan Fort underwent during the first century BC. At this stage a huge circular structure was erected, although its exact role still remains a mystery. It was supported on approximately 275 posts, each one thicker than a telegraph pole, and at its centre stood the trunk of a single oak, which was more than 0.5 metres (1½ feet) thick. Tests have shown that the latter was originally felled in 94 BC.

This extraordinary building was never used as a dwelling, much less as a palace. Within a few years of its completion, the interior was filled with a cairn of limestone blocks. The entire place was then set on fire, apparently deliberately, and the charred remains covered with a mound of turf. The whole undertaking has been interpreted as a sacrificial rite on a grand scale, even though its precise purpose cannot be ascertained.

The sheer scale of Navan Fort makes it the most impressive architectural feat of the early Celtic era, underlining the degree of communal cooperation that these people could achieve. Certainly its reputation as a holy place must have lingered on, because it can surely be no coincidence that St Patrick chose to make nearby Armagh his own spiritual base.

CHAPTER THREE

THE FIVE · KINGDOMS

By the fifth century AD, five independent provinces, or *Cóiceda*, were recognized by the ancient Celts, ruled over by petty kings and peopled by different tribes. Inter-tribal warfare became commonplace and borders shifted and changed as the battles raged. The military prowess of the Celts is legendary and many of the battles related in the tales of the Ulster Cycle have some foundation in fact.

GRIANÁN OF AILEACH, COUNTY DONEGAL
This striking hill-fort was once the chief stronghold of the O'Loughlins, a branch of the northern Uí Néill.

THE FIVE KINGDOMS

IN IRELAND, AS IN SO many other parts of the Celtic world, the cohesion that was evident in social and cultural matters was noticeably absent from the political sphere. However well it might function on a local level, the *tuath* (or tribe) was none the less a very small political unit, and petty kingships soon began to proliferate. One medieval source stated that Irish kings were as commonplace as counts in any other country, and it has been estimated that, at any given time, there may have been as many as 150 different kings ruling in Ireland. The fortunes of these early kingships are hard to determine. There are no firm dates in Irish history before the fifth century AD. Prior to this events were recorded in a pot-pourri of legends, pseudo-histories and genealogical lists, which were conveyed orally over a long period of time and cannot be verified.

The oldest tribal groupings are usually distinguished by the linguistic origins of their name. Most of these names consist of a general term for 'people', combined with an ancestor figure, a totem figure or a local deity. The most widely used examples of the former are *Dál* ('the share of'), *Corco* ('the seed of') and the suffix *-raige* ('the people of'). Totem figures were normally animals, giving rise to such tribal names as the Osraige ('deer-people'), Sordraige ('boar-people') and Grecraige ('horse-people'). In some cases, the names related to animals that were not even present in Ireland (the Bibraige or 'beaver-people', for instance), suggesting a distant continental ancestry for the tribe.

SWORD HILT
This bronze hilt was retrieved from Ballyshannon Bay, County Donegal. The anthropoid design is typically La Tène and probably dates from the first century BC.

Similarly, some of the most ancient clans incorporated the names of Irish gods into their own names. Typical examples include the Boandraige, worshippers of Bóann, the water-goddess who is commemorated in the name of the River Boyne, and the Luigne, who were devotees of the sun-god Lugh. It is possible that reference to such divinities signified more than simply worship of them, and was meant to indicate that the tribe regarded these deities as their ancestors. Certainly, the use of ancestor names became increasingly common, and most of the

tribes that survived into the historic era derived their name from a forefather.

Ultimately, the most powerful of these tribes grew into confederations, linked by a common ancestor. Again, this shift in emphasis is most evident in linguistic terms. The new factions were known by such names as *Uí* ('grand-children'), *Cenél* ('kindred'), *Síl* ('offspring') and *Clann* ('family'). Strictly speaking, these terms refer to the main ruling dynasties, rather than to actual tribes.

The Cóiceda

On a broader scale, these dynasties competed for control of the *Cóiceda* ('Fifths'), the five main kingdoms of early Ireland. These were roughly equivalent to the modern provinces of Leinster, Ulster, Munster and Connaught,

together with *Mide* ('Middle') – a central kingdom which consisted of the counties of Meath and Westmeath, along with some adjacent territory. These ancient divisions date back to prehistoric times, but there is no way of knowing precisely when they came into being. The dates set down in genealogies or ancestor myths vary dramatically, from region to region. Nor did they remain fixed divisions throughout Ireland's early history. The fortunes of individual tribes and families fluctuated constantly, and with them the territorial boundaries of each of the provinces.

Hints of the changing nature of these power blocs can be found in various literary sources. In the admittedly partisan stories about Cú Chulainn, the emphasis is on the war between Ulster and Connacht. These appear to be the most powerful forces in the whole land, and there is no suggestion that either of their leaders owes allegiance to a higher king. In the Fionn Cycle, however, a different situation is reflected. These later tales, supposedly set in the third century AD, revolve around the adventures of Fionn mac Cumhaill (or Finn mac Cool, see p.50) and his knightly companions. They are based at the court of Cormac mac Airt, an early king of Tara, which is portrayed as the most important princely centre in Ireland – a foretaste of the position that it would hold as the seat of the high kings.

The Book of Invasions (see p.30), meanwhile, provides a third scenario, recording that only the Connachta and the Eóganachta of Munster were directly descended from Míl, the ancestor of the Milesian race. Since the latter were widely regarded as the founders of the Irish people, it followed that these two tribes were deemed superior to all the others. It also reflected another common belief – namely, that the real contest for power in early Ireland lay between the northern and southern halves of the country, rather than between the five kingdoms. These two territories, divided along a line that stretched from Galway Bay to the future site of Dublin, were known as the *Leth Cuinn* ('Conn's half') in the north and the *Leth Moga* ('Mug's half') in the south, after the legendary founders of two of the principal ruling dynasties.

HILL OF USHNAGH, COUNTY WESTMEATH
According to legend, the Middle Kingdom was founded in c. AD 130 by Tuathal Teachmhair, one of the early high kings. He chose the Hill of Ushnagh as the core of his new province.

The Eóganachta of the South

Mug Nuadat ('Servant of Nuadu'), who was also known as Eógan Mór, was an ancestor of the Eóganachta, the dominant force in Munster. The Nuadu in question was an Irish god, consort of the water-goddess Bóann, and the 'founder' of a number of Irish tribes. Mug did battle with the northern leader, Conn Cétchathach, on several occasions, and it was after one such clash that the central dividing line was supposedly drawn up. By and large, Conn appears to have come off worst in the various conflicts and, for a time, was forced to seek refuge in Spain. He returned, however, to take part in the Battle of Mag Léna (now Kilbride, County Offaly), where he was killed. The traditional date for this clash is AD 137 but, as with all material for this era, both the battle and its date were probably invented by later annalists.

THE FIVE KINGDOMS

Ulster

Connacht

Middle
Kingdom

Leinster

Munster

**ROCK OF CASHEL,
COUNTY TIPPERARY**

Part citadel and part cathedral, Cashel was the ancient stronghold of the Eóganachta. It remained primarily a secular site until the twelfth century, when Muircheartach O'Brien bestowed it on the Church.

The Eóganachta take their name from Mug's grandson, Eógan. Very little is known about him, although it has been suggested that one of the legendary battles linked with his name (Cenn Abrat) may actually have been a folk memory of a genuine clash with Erainn invaders (the Erainn were a historical Celtic people, who began arriving in Ireland in the fifth century BC). The most celebrated figure in the prehistoric lore of the Eóganachta, however, was Conall Corc, who was said to have founded Cashel, County Tipperary, the chief stronghold and future capital of Munster. According to legend, he was exiled in Britain for a time and, on his return, witnessed a vision of a yew tree sprouting from a stone. Immediately his druids instructed him to kindle a fire upon this stone, since this would guarantee that his descendants would be kings of Munster for evermore. If he existed at all, Conall probably lived in the early fifth century AD, but the first ruler of the Eóganachta who can be identified with any certainty is Oengus, a king of Cashel who died in 490.

The Connachta of the North

To the north, meanwhile, Munster's traditional rivals were the Connachta, the tribe that gave its name to the modern province of Connaught. They were called after their ancestor-deity figure, Conn Cétchathach ('Conn of the Hundred Battles'), who bested Mug Nuadat in a series of clashes, lending his name to the northern division of the country (*Leth Cuinn*, or Conn's half). He also seized Tara for himself, deposing the Leinster king Cathair Mór. Conn Cétchathach featured prominently in the myths surrounding Fionn mac Cumhaill – in most versions of the tales he was cited as the king of Tara at the time of Fionn's birth – although there were contradictory accounts in the Fionn Cycle about his character. In some versions of the tales it was reported that Conn had killed Fionn's father; in others that the two men fought alongside each other as allies.

FOLLOWING PAGE – DUNGUIRE CASTLE, COUNTY GALWAY
This picturesque castle was built on the site where Guaire,
a seventh-century king of Connacht, once had his stronghold.

THREE-FACED HEAD OF A CELTIC DEITY
*The number three had particular significance in
Celtic religion.*

At a later stage the Connachta split into three main
groups, the Uí Briúin, the Uí Maine and the Uí Fiachrach.
The Uí Briúin had settlements along the banks of the River
Shannon, particularly in the lowlands east of Loch Mask;
the Uí Fiachrach were based in northern Mayo; while the
Uí Maine held parts of present-day County Roscommon
and County Galway. The kingship of Connacht tended to
rotate between these three, each of which paid reverence
to their ancestor figures. The chief heroes of the Uí Maine
were Marcán, who is thought to have been the prototype
of the Cornish King Mark of Arthurian legend, and Eochu
Rond, who fought a duel with Cú Chulainn. For the Uí
Fiachrach, the most important ruler was Guaire, a genuine
historical figure who died in 663. In addition to his victories in the field, he became a byword for generosity and
kindness, acquiring the nickname 'Guaire of the extended
hand'. The later stronghold of Dún Guaire, County
Galway, was named in his honour. Finally, among the Uí
Briúin the most prominent leader was Aed, son of Eochu
Tirmcharna, who won a notable victory at the Battle of
Cúil Dreimne, before meeting his death in 577.

The Ulaid of Ulster

The Connachta had strong connections with the neigh-
bouring people of Ulster, who took their name from the
Ulaid, a term that describes both a tribe and its territory.
Originally a warrior caste of La Tène Celts who had

migrated from Britain, the Ulaid gained lasting fame through the stories in the Ulster Cycle that described how their champion, Cú Chulainn, vanquished the invading forces of Connacht. The Ulaid, at this period, were at the peak of their influence. In the west, their power extended as far as Sligo Bay, while to the south they occupied most

COOLEY PENINSULA, COUNTY LOUTH
A famous name in Irish literature. It was from this fertile region that Queen Maeve stole a magical bull, as a result of which war broke out with Ulster.

FIONN MAC CUMHAILL AND THE FIANNA

Cú Chulainn, the champion of Ulster, epitomizes the values of Ireland's heroic age: his feats of strength, his courage and his valiant duels with the enemy confirm his status as an individual with superhuman qualities. In no sense can he be classed as a team player. The stories about Fionn mac Cumhaill and the Fianna, however, belong to a different era. Set in the third century AD, they relate the exploits of a group of noble warriors, bound by a common code of conduct. As such, they have often been cited as precursors of King Arthur and the Knights of the Round Table.

The Fianna (plural of *fian*, a 'warrior') were a military élite whose members underwent strict training and had to perform hazardous initiation tests before they could be accepted into the band. The leader of the group was Fionn mac Cumhaill, who proved his worthiness for the post by avenging his father's death and acquiring the Treasure Bag of the Fianna (a magical crane-skin bag containing the weapons of the sea-god, Manannán mac Lir). The most notable members of the Fianna were Oisín, Oscar and Diarmaid. Oisín, Fionn's son, was renowned for his adventures in Tir na nOg, a land of eternal youth, where he dwelt for 300 years with Niamh of the Golden Hair. Oscar was the greatest warrior in the company, an Irish equivalent of Sir Galahad. Diarmaid eloped with Fionn's betrothed, Gráinne, and the couple were forced to spend sixteen years on the run, before being rescued by Oenghus, the god of love.

of the territories of what would later become the Middle Kingdom. Their 'capital', Emain Macha (now Navan Fort, see p.38, 39), was also celebrated in the *Táin Bó Cuailgne* (The Cattle Raid of Cooley), and subsequent excavations have confirmed that this was indeed a place of great ritual significance.

In spite of all these glories, the power of the Ulaid shrank considerably before the end of the Iron Age. By then, the Ulster *cóiced* ('fifth') had split into three, with the Ulaid confined to the eastern section. Precisely how this happened is far from clear. The pseudo-histories relate how a mysterious tribe known as the Airgialla ('Hostage-givers') seized the central portion of the

province, destroying the stronghold of Emain Macha in the process. Their leaders in this campaign were three brothers (possibly one of many triads of gods) known as the Three Collas, who claimed descent from Conn Cétchathach. Meanwhile, the western segment of the kingdom was seized by the northern branch of the Uí Néill, who created a new capital of Ulster at Aileach. Some aspects of this account have been rejected: archaeologists have shown that Emain Macha was not destroyed in the course of a military campaign, and many authorities are convinced that – as their name suggests – the Airgialla were actually a subject-people, dominated by the neighbouring Uí Néill.

The Uí Néill Dynasty

The Uí Néill were the first of the great Irish dynasties. They took their name from Niall Noígiallach ('Niall of the Nine Hostages'), one of the most controversial figures of ancient Ireland. Some have described him as the first genuinely historical high king, claiming that he ruled from AD 379 to 405. This may be so, but the details of his life are obscured by a welter of legends. He was said to have been the son of a British slave-girl, abandoned at birth on a remote hillside and raised by a wandering bard. As an adult, he was deemed to have led raiding parties into Britain and Gaul, and one source has even suggested that one of these sorties involved the abduction of St Patrick from his British homeland. The traditional explanation of his colourful nickname is that he demanded a hostage from all five kingdoms of Ireland, together with one each from the British, the French, the Scots and the Saxons. If such hostage-taking took place, however, it is much more likely that Niall's prisoners were taken from the nine *tuatha* of Airgialla. Either way, the unfortunate captives gave their name to one of the best-known features of the prehistoric remains at Tara, the so-called 'Mound of the Hostages'.

Niall is believed to have had fourteen or fifteen sons, who spearheaded the creation of eight new kingdoms. These came under the auspices of the family's two main branches, the northern and southern Uí Néill. The northern branch of the dynasty made most of its advances at the expense of the Ulaid. There were also links with the Connachta, with whom they shared a common ancestor – Conn Cétchathach. In addition, Niall's brothers included

Brión (founder of the Uí Briúin) and Fiachra (founder of the Uí Fiachrach). The southern Uí Néill, meanwhile, seized Tara and made deep inroads into the Middle Kingdom. For the next few centuries, one branch or other of the dynasty would invariably hold the post of high king.

The Middle Kingdom

The genesis of this Middle Kingdom is particularly hard to trace. Its legendary founder was Tuathal Teachmhair, who is said to have ruled as high king from AD 130 to 160 and to have been the grandfather of Conn Cétchathach. According to tradition, Tuathal arrived in Ireland at the head of a group of Goidelic invaders, carving out his new domain by taking segments from each of the four existing provinces.

More probably, the core of the *cóiced* was built up around the Hill of Ushnagh, County Westmeath. This mystical site had long been regarded as the navel – the very centre of Ireland. From its heights, the viewer could look down on to each of the other provinces. Its importance is confirmed by the fact that it bears the remains of a major ritual site, that it was the venue for a large *óenach* (annual assembly), and that ceremonial fires were kindled there at the Celtic festival of Beltane. The *Book of Invasions* contains an account explaining that this rite was inspired by a druid named Mide, who had accompanied the Nemedians (see p.30) on their invasion of Ireland. Upon his arrival at the Hill of Ushnagh, Mide lit a flame that burned brightly for seven years, and from which every other fire in Ireland was lit.

The Middle Kingdom was to hold considerable symbolic significance for potential invaders, as the seat of the *ard rí*, or 'high king'. This significance belongs to the historic period, from approximately the fifth century AD in Ireland, although later annalists were swift to stress the antiquity of the office. Surviving bardic king-lists name no fewer than 107 high kings who reigned in the BC era – among them nine Fir Bolgs, nine members of the Tuatha Dé Danaan and eighty-nine Milesians.

THE BOOK OF KELLS
This intricate calligraphy comes from the most famous Celtic manuscript, the Book of Kells. *The initial letters are formed from a network of animal tongues, ears and tails.*

> ' *Now Cú Chulainn's battle-fury came upon him. His entire body began to quiver violently, like a willow bough in a gale or a reed caught in a torrent. The rage turned his face into a sickening mask of red, throbbing flesh. One eye sank back so far inside his skull that a wild crane could have flown into the space and hidden there, while the other dangled on his cheek like a soft fruit. His hair curled snake-like on his head and, above it, the air turned to a boiling mist with the heat of his fury. A light shone out from his forehead, bright as a halo, and sprays of smoke-black blood spurted from the top of his skull.* '
>
> THE CATTLE RAID OF COOLEY
> *from the Ulster Cycle*

The Laigin of Leinster

While the Uí Néill came to dominate the kingship of Tara, their power was frequently contested by the Laigin, the early inhabitants of Leinster. They are thought to be one of the most ancient races of Celtic invaders, second only to the Erainn. Their ancestor figure was Labraid Loingsech or Labraid Móen, a legendary prince who was tormented by Cobhthach, his evil uncle. Cobhthach slew Labraid's father and forced the boy to eat his heart, an ordeal that robbed the young prince of the power of speech. Seeking revenge, he enlisted the assistance of a force of Gaulish warriors, who helped him to depose Cobhthach, and it was from the Gauls' distinctive broad spears (*laighne*) that the name Laigin derived.

It is quite possible that the Laigin were genuinely of Gaulish origin, but they were not the only Celtic tribe to

STAIGUE FORT, COUNTY KERRY
These are the remains of one of Ireland's most impressive hill-forts. Its main function was to serve as a stronghold, although it is possible that it was also used as a staging post for pilgrims travelling to the nearby island of Skellig Michael.

settle in Leinster. Two other invading groups have also been identified. These are the Fir Domnann (thought to be a race of P-Celts originating from Britain) and the Galióin. The latter are often associated with the Fir Bolg, an ancient race of invaders, although they have also been seen as an archaic form of the Laigin themselves. They are mentioned in the *Táin*, where a powerful contingent of Galióin warriors ally themselves with the Connacht army, ready to pit their skills against Cú Chulainn.

The Leinstermen appear to have had their own 'royal' site at Dún Ailinne – an important ritual centre, comparable in many ways to Emain Macha – and also had their share of legendary heroes. These include Cathair Mór, an ancestral king deposed by Conn Cétchathach; and Find File, a poet-king who is said to have resided at Dún Ailinne. Find File is sometimes confused with Fionn mac Cumhaill, leader of the Fianna: the names of both came from the same root (meaning 'fair') and even their homes sounded similar (Fionn dwelt in a stronghold on the Hill of Allen).

A high percentage of the copious annals on Leinster's history deal with the Laigin's struggles against their powerful neighbours. To the west, they were shielded to some extent by the petty kingdoms of the Loígis and the Osraige (the latter giving their name to the modern diocese of Ossory in County Kilkenny). To the north, however, there was increasing rivalry between the Laigin and the southern Uí Néill over the possession of Tara and the Middle Kingdom. Propagandists for the Uí Néill cause claimed that their dynasty held an effective monopoly on the kingship of Tara, but the Laigin annalists also reported a few successful claimants. The most notable of these was Bresal Bélach, who was said to have fought alongside Fionn mac Cumhaill and the Fianna at the Battle of Cnámross.

Open Warfare

Surviving records list an extremely lengthy sequence of battles between the two parties during the second half of the fifth century. These began in 452–3, when the Laigin suffered two crushing defeats at the hands of their enemies, and continued until 516, when the Uí Néill won a decisive victory at Druim Derg, which finally gave them permanent control over the Middle Kingdom. As usual, both the names and the dates of the battles are open to question, but there is no disputing the sheer volume of fighting that went on. Warfare was endemic in the early Celtic kingdoms, and it left its mark on every aspect of daily life.

The methods and attitudes of Celtic warriors are well documented, both by classical authors and in the early Irish sagas, and this has enabled scholars to gain a fuller understanding of the relationship between the Iron Age Celts in Ireland and their counterparts in continental Europe. For the ancient Greeks and Romans, initial contact with the Celts often came on the battlefield, so classical writers paid great attention to their military prowess.

In general, the Celts were found to be brave, ferocious and boastful, but somewhat unsubtle in their tactics. An account by the Greek geographer Strabo (64 BC–after AD 24) is typical:

The whole race is madly fond of war, high-spirited and quick for battle, but otherwise uncomplicated and not of evil character. When they are stirred up in this way, they tend to rush into battle all together, without concealment or forethought, and so can be handled easily by those who mean to outwit them... Once provoked, they are willing to risk everything, even if they have nothing to rely on other than their own strength and courage.

Many authors noted that Celtic warriors had no apparent fear of death. This was partly the result of their religious beliefs – most notably, their convictions about the transmigration of the soul – and partly because they made deliberate attempts to fight in a frenzied state, in a manner comparable to that of the Norse berserkers. This practice was certainly adopted in Ireland. Several passages in the *Táin* describe how Cú Chulainn would assume an extraordinary 'battle-fury' before going out to meet the enemy. Invariably this frenzy endowed him with superhuman strength and endurance.

Taunts, challenges and boasts also formed a necessary part of the preliminaries. To the Romans, this appeared to be nothing more than vainglorious bragging, but these rituals were an essential part of the Celtic code of honour. In the *Táin*, on numerous occasions, Cú Chulainn set his adversaries difficult challenges – performing a feat of strength, perhaps, or a tricky manoeuvre on a chariot – and they were duty-bound to attempt them. This kind of test was linked to Celtic notions about taboos (see p.95).

The Tools of Battle

In material terms, the Celts relied heavily on two things: their chariots (see p.61) and their long, heavy swords. In his *De Bello Gallico* (The Gallic Wars, published in 51BC), Julius Caesar (100–44 BC) noted how they used their chariots to create a sense of panic:

First they career around in every direction, hurling their spears. The fear inspired by the horses and the din of the wheels is usually enough to unsettle the opposition. Then they leap off their chariots to fight on foot, while the chariot drivers withdraw, ready to return when necessary… In this way, they combine the mobility of cavalry with the solidity of infantry.

This tallies closely with the actions of Cú Chulainn and the Ulstermen in the *Táin*.

Many Celtic tribes made use of heavy, iron swords. These had long, tapering blades with sharp edges but a blunt end. They proved particularly effective when wielded as a slashing weapon by lines of charging horsemen. Even the Romans, who were accustomed to short, stabbing swords, were initially concerned by the devastating force of such weapons. However, they countered the threat by strengthening their shields and using long spears to keep the swordsmen at bay. Because of their blunt tips, Celtic swords could not function as thrusting weapons, and their weight made them cumbersome in hand-to-hand combat.

Military Forts

Tangible evidence of this kind of military activity can be found in the many ruined forts scattered throughout the Irish countryside, and in the examples of weaponry that have been discovered at archaeological sites. The standard Irish word for a stronghold was a *dún*, and this features extensively in many place-names. Dundalk in County Louth, for example, is derived from *Dún Delga* (Delga's stronghold). Nothing concrete is known about this Delga, although he is sometimes supposed to have been a chieftain of the Fomorians, one of the ancient races that invaded Ireland in prehistoric times. It was common practice for later generations to ascribe the

Cú Chulainn learns the arts of war from Scáthach, a mystical female warrior:

She taught him how to juggle nine apples in the air, hurling each in turn at approaching foes; she showed him how to balance on the point of a spear or the rim of a shield; she tutored him in the hero's scream, which could make an enemy fall dead on the spot; she taught him the thunder-feat, the cat's feat and the rope-feat. He learned how to ride a sickle-chariot and how to catch a javelin in full flight.

THE CATTLE RAID OF COOLEY
from the Táin Bó Cuailgene

remains of great fortresses to mythical kings or heroes. Accordingly, *Dún Delga* eventually became associated with Cú Chulainn, the champion of Ulster. In the *Táin* and other stories it is described as his principal home.

The *dún* was not exclusive to Ireland, and similar examples can be found throughout the Celtic world. In Wales it was known as a *dinas*, as in Dinas Emrys (the stronghold of Emrys Wledig, who led his people against the Saxons). Similarly, in those parts of continental Europe that were conquered by the Romans, it was latinized as the suffix *dunum*. Thus the French city of Lyons was called Lugdunum, or 'the stronghold of Lugh' (the Celtic sun-god and the father of Cú Chulainn).

Broadly speaking, the more powerful Irish military forts fall into two main categories: those that relied on a single line of defence, and those that were multivallate (that is, having a series of ramparts). In both cases the builders took pains to extract every possible advantage from the landscape, seeking sites that were easy to defend. Their favourite locations were hilltops or promontories jutting out into the sea.

One of the best-preserved examples of a hilltop stronghold is Staigue Fort in County Kerry. Situated at the head of a valley on the Iveragh peninsula, it is composed of a simple, circular stone enclosure, with walls that are almost 4 metres (13 feet) thick and an internal diameter of some 24 metres (78 feet). The walls incline slightly inwards.

making life doubly difficult for any potential attackers, and defenders had the added protection of two passageways, set within the walls. Staigue is thought to have been built during the Iron Age, but it remained in use during the Christian era, when it provided a staging post for pilgrims travelling to Skellig Michael, a famous monastic centre in the far west of the province.

Dun Aenghus –
Fort of the Fir Bolg?

Of the surviving multivallate fortresses, the most spectacular example is Dun Aenghus, in County Galway. It is particularly impressive on account of its precipitous position, perched on top of a cliff-face on Inishmore, the largest of the three Aran islands. Inaccessible from the sea, its landward side is protected by three horseshoe-shaped ramparts, together with the remnants of a fourth. The innermost wall is again around 4 metres (13 feet) thick and, like the other forts, it is honeycombed with a number of tiny chambers. The most distinctive feature of its defences, however, is the *chevaux-de-frise* ('Friesian horses'). This is the name given to a row of stone spikes, which would have impeded the approach of any attacking warriors, particularly those on horseback. Dun Aenghus is one of only four Irish forts to be protected by *chevaux-de-frise*, all of them situated in the western part of the country. This has given rise to a theory that the stronghold was built by invaders from the Iberian peninsula, where this type of defence was more common. The notion is an intriguing one, but there is no firm evidence to support it.

As with most of the forts of this kind, the early history of Dun Aenghus remains a mystery. According to the Book of Invasions, it was thought to have been built by the Fir Bolg and named after one of their chiefs. In reality, the only worthwhile hint about its origins was provided by a bronze La Tène fibula (brooch) which was

DUN AENGHUS, COUNTY GALWAY
This stunning promontory fort is set in a dizzying position, on the brink of a sheer cliff-face. Its landward side was protected by the chevaux-de-frise, *seen here in the foreground, which hindered the advance of approaching enemies just as they came within range of the defenders' slings.*

discovered in 1839 by a group of boys hunting for rabbits in the inner enclosure of the fort. This lends support to the widely held belief that the fort dates back to the Celtic Iron Age.

The commanding, strategic position of Dun Aenghus underlines its military character, but with other Irish forts the position is more ambiguous. There has been a suggestion, for example, that some hill-forts were deliberately erected on the site of earlier burial mounds, in order to gain a measure of spiritual protection from the sanctified nature of the place. This is possible, but by no means certain.

In some instances the main attraction appears to have been the ready availability of building material. At Freestone Hill, County Kilkenny, for example, Celtic tribesmen dismantled the cairns of earlier Bronze Age burial sites, using the stones to construct their fort.

Only a few of the ancient Irish strongholds can be linked with any confidence to historical figures or events. The Grianán (literally 'sunny place') of Aileach, a much-restored hill-fort in County Donegal, has typically obscure beginnings. Traditionally, its construction is ascribed to the Tuatha Dé Danaan (the Irish gods), but its later history is rather more secure. In c. 425 AD, it was said to have been appropriated by Eógan, son of Niall of the Nine Hostages. He founded the O'Loughlins, a branch of the northern Ui Néill dynasty (Niall's descendants), who became the hereditary kings of Aileach. The stronghold was also recognized as the 'capital' of Ulster, following the destruction of Emain Macha.

Similarly, the massive fort of Dún Ailinne, County Kildare – one of the largest in Ireland – is widely regarded as the chief seat of the kings of Leinster. Modern excavations (1968–74) indicate a human presence dating right back to Neolithic times, although the main activity there took place during the Iron Age.

Between the third or second century BC and the second century AD, a succession of large timber palisades was erected, which seem to have been used for ritual purposes, rather than for habitation. Along with a number of La Tène artefacts (armlets, fibulae and a sword), archaeologists discovered more than 18,000 fragments of animal bone, which may be the residue of ceremonial feasting. For reasons that remain unclear, the site appears to have been abandoned during the Early Christian period.

Ireland is richly endowed with remains of ancient forts and strongholds, but by comparison finds of Celtic weaponry and military paraphernalia have been rather disappointing. Most items from the Hallstatt era (see p.25) appear to be imports (or copies of imports), and even discoveries of La Tène artefacts (see pp.25–6) have been rather sparse. Nevertheless, there is still enough material to give a vivid impression of soldiering in the heroic age.

Warrior Weapons

The finest individual pieces are certainly the scabbards found at Lisnacrogher, County Antrim, and the River Bann (see p.60), which display the graceful, curvilinear patterns that are typical of the mature La Tène style. The strength of these designs, and the quantity of items found in this region, suggest that there must have been a specialist school of armourers in the north-eastern part of the country.

Elsewhere, the finds are intriguing rather than spectacular. In the harbour of Ballyshannon Bay, County Donegal, an anthropoid sword-hilt (one shaped like the figure of a man, see p.42) was dredged up. The figure's bulging, stylized features are typical of the late La Tène style, but quite unlike anything else found in Ireland. Almost certainly, this weapon was brought across from western Gaul.

On the whole, Irish swords were shorter than their heavier continental counterparts, making them marginally more suitable for hand-to-hand combat, although still not effective as thrusting weapons against the Romans. The most complete example is probably the iron sword discovered at the lakeside settlement of Ballinderry, County Offaly.

Spear-butts and spearheads may have less visual appeal, but they reflect an important aspect of Irish warfare. The Celts were especially fond of using spears and javelins, and they played a correspondingly large part in the ancient myths. Cú Chulainn's favourite weapon was the gae bolga, a fearsome casting spear that was made from the bones of a sea-monster. Once it had penetrated the skin of an opponent the spear's head opened out, creating a further thirty wounds. Other tales describe magical spears which took on a life of their own. In *Oidheadh Chlainne Tuireann* (The Fate of the Children of Tuireann), part of the Mythological Cycle, King Pezar owned one called 'The Slaughterer', which had a fiery point and had to be kept in a cauldron of water in case it burned down the royal palace. Similarly, Keltchar of the Battles possessed a spear called *Lúin* ('lance'), which was notorious for its blood-lust. Whenever he entered a fray, the weapon would shake in his hand, desperate for the taste of flesh. At other times, Keltchar would soak its tip in a cauldron of black venom, to satiate its perverse appetite and prevent it from attacking any bystanders.

Irish spears came in two basic forms, the casting spear and the thrusting spear, although both were subject to considerable variation. This can be deduced from the number of different words for the weapon (among others, *gae*, *foga* and *sleg*) and for distinctive types of spearhead. Some of these were extremely long, measuring as much as 90 centimetres (36 inches), and the finest ones had engraved decoration on the blade. The butts were small, cylindrical tubes, fitted to the end of the shaft to prevent it from splintering. These, too, might be decorated with engraved patterns or enamel inlays, or formed into different shapes. The most elaborate examples have a bulbous terminal, similar to a doorknob.

While fragments of swords and spears are in plentiful supply, finds of other forms of military equipment are surprisingly rare. Metal shields, for example, are virtually unknown. The most important discovery in this field is a circular bronze shield which came to light at Lough Gur, County Limerick. It consists of a thin sheet of metal, decorated with six circular ridges, separated by rows of hemispherical bosses. This design served an entirely practical purpose. A plain sheet of bronze would have been either too fragile to withstand repeated sword strokes or, if thicker, too heavy to wield effectively. A corrugated surface, however, could deflect an enemy's blows with far greater ease.

The Lough Gur shield is very early, dating back to the Dowris phase (c. 700 BC). During the Celtic era most warriors appear to have switched to shields made out of organic materials, such as wood or leather, and these have mostly perished. One remarkable exception is the rectangular shield that was preserved in Littleton Bog near Clonoura, County

SHIELD AND SCABBARD

The bronze scabbards discovered at Lisnacrogher, County Antrim, feature intricate leaf-and-spiral decoration. The shield from Lough Gur, County Limerick (left), is made out of sheet bronze and dates from the Dowris phase (c. 700 BC).

Tipperary. It was made from alderwood and covered in lengths of calf-hide. A domed wooden boss at the centre protected the hand-grip. The front of the shield bears the marks of several sword strokes, proving that it was used in battle, unlike the more elaborate, ceremonial examples that have been discovered in Britain.

Shields of this kind were frequently adorned with a metal boss. This might take the form of the warrior's totem figure or a conventional symbol of war, such as a boar. In many cases, however, they were nothing more than plain, metal discs. The bronze boss that was retrieved from a cemetery on Lambay Island, County Dublin, is a typical example. On some occasions warriors kept a hand-stone in the hollow of their shield, ready to hurl at the enemy at an appropriate moment. These stones, which were known by a number of different names (for example, *cloch*, *lec*, and *lia*), were thought to possess a malign and mystical quality.

Slings, Helmets and Chariots of War

Stones were also propelled by means of slings, a favourite weapon among Irish warriors. Their widespread use is confirmed by the frequent references to them in early literature. Cú Chulainn used one extensively in the *Táin*, for example, harassing the Connacht army at night by picking off their sentries with his slingshots. The Irish used two types of sling: the simple *teilm*, which consisted of two thongs stitched on to a piece of leather, and the *crann-taball* ('wood-sling'), which combined a long staff with the thongs. The original slings have of course long since disappeared, but stores of rounded stones – clearly intended as slingshots – have often been found at early homesteads.

LISNACROGHER

The richest finds of Irish weaponry have been made in County Antrim. The River Bann and the marshy site at Lisnacrogher have yielded up no fewer than eight bronze scabbards, together with an iron sword, a decorated spearhead and a variety of related metal fittings. Sadly, the importance of these discoveries has been somewhat devalued by the damage caused to the original site.

The treasures of Lisnacrogher were uncovered at the end of the nineteenth century, during the course of routine peat-cutting. Before the site could be properly evaluated, however, it was ransacked by local collectors. One, in particular, used to boast that he never left his house without 'carrying back something to enrich his collection'. Since he did not keep a proper record of the objects, or of the precise location in which he found them, the dating and interpretation of the hoard have been problematic.

The likeliest explanation is that Lisnacrogher was originally a crannog – an artificial island – built on top of the watery site. Early accounts describe the remains of timber posts and compacted brushwood, which might have formed the foundations of just such a dwelling. However, it is also feasible that this was a sacred place where expensive artefacts were deposited, as gifts for the gods. The Celts invariably chose rivers or marshy sites for these offerings, sometimes constructing wooden causeways across them. If Lisnacrogher did have a religious purpose, this would explain the high quality of the finds and the absence of cheaper domestic items.

The most important discoveries at Lisnacrogher were the scabbards, adorned with flowing arrangements of S-shaped curves and spirals. Their basic patterns were marked out with compasses, while the more extravagant flourishes were drawn freehand. They correspond closely in appearance with Celtic weapons produced on the continent during the third century BC, although this style may have reached Ireland at a slightly later date.

PETRIE CROWN
This remarkable head-dress is one of the most sophisticated examples of La Tène metalworking. It dates from the first century AD.

Helmets are equally rare. The only finds of any note are the Petrie Crown and the Cork horn head-dress, both of which were undoubtedly ceremonial items that were never actually worn in battle. The Petrie Crown, which is named after one of its earliest owners, the antiquary George Petrie (1789–1866), is one of the greatest glories of Irish La Tène. Its low-relief designs combine trumpet spirals with stylized, crested bird's heads. Only one of its horns has survived (originally there would have been two); it was created by folding a sheet of metal into the desired shape and then riveting it into place. The pattern was added to the horn after it was already *in situ*, which must have required immense technical skill. The triple-horned head-dress discovered in 1909 by the River Lee in Cork displays a very similar style. Like the Petrie Crown, it was probably attached to perishable materials which have long since vanished.

Helmets are mentioned only in passing in the early literature, which may raise doubts about the extent of their use, but the same cannot be said for chariots. From the Ulster Cycle and other heroic sagas, it is clear that the two-man chariot was an essential piece of equipment for Iron Age chieftains.

Despite this, archaeological finds have been very meagre. There appear to be two reasons for this. First, the Irish did not carry out chariot-burials, in contrast to tribes in certain other parts of Celtic Europe. Second, Irish chariots seem to have been composed almost entirely of wood, with very few metal fittings (mostly mounts and linchpins). They do not even seem to have needed metal terrets – the rings through which the reins were passed. Instead, the reins appear to have been passed through holes in the yoke. Only one bronze terret has so far been found in Ireland, and even this was probably a British import.

War Trumpets

Perhaps the most impressive of all the military finds in Ireland are the richly adorned examples of a *carnyx* or war trumpet. Throughout the Celtic world warriors used to make a deafening din as they went into battle, hoping that this would unsettle their opponents. Their favourite means of doing so was a long-stemmed trumpet, which sometimes took the form of an open-mouthed boar. The largest and best-preserved of the Irish trumpets comes from Ardbrin, County Down. It is 1.42 metres (over 4½ feet) long and its elaborate construction entailed the use of no fewer than 1,094 rivets. Another example, this time from Loughnashade, County Armagh, is only slightly shorter and features a greater degree of decoration. Its mouth terminates in a flattened ring, which features a repoussé design of flowing tendrils and interlocking spirals.

The Loughnashade find was made in 1798, when four bronze trumpets and a number of human skulls were fished out of a tiny lake, close to the site of Emain Macha. In all probability, they formed part of a lavish (if somewhat gruesome) ritual sacrifice. Offerings of this kind were commonplace in the La Tène era, confirming the very high regard that the ancient Celts had for finely wrought weapons and military equipment.

BRONZE HORN
The Celts used horns and trumpets to strike fear into the hearts of their opponents as they went into battle.

CHAPTER FOUR

MYTHOLOGY AND RELIGION

Any study of Celtic religion is hampered by three main factors. For centuries the learning of the Celts was transmitted orally, rather than through the written word. As a result, the few contemporary accounts of their practices that have survived come mainly from their enemies, who could report only from an outsider's point of view. Second, there is a comparable scarcity of visual clues. Most La Tène art, for example, consisted of semi-abstract pattern-making and there was little attempt to produce realistic, figurative images. Only a handful of carvings of Celtic deities are known, and these originate from continental Europe, rather than from Ireland. Finally, those cultures that superseded the Celts often had a vested interest in destroying the heritage of their predecessors.

BEN BULBEN, COUNTY SLIGO
The misty summit of this mountain was a place of ill omen. Hapless Diarmaid died here, after being gored by a bull.

MYTHOLOGY AND RELIGION

IRELAND AT LEAST fared better than its continental counterparts in this last respect. Throughout much of Europe the Romans made strenuous efforts to obliterate Celtic influences, replacing them with the values of their own civilization. The Irish escaped this fate – Celtic religious practices survived until the coming of Christianity and, even then, the destruction of La Tène influences was not total. For while the missionaries obviously had no desire to preserve pagan beliefs, they did copy down the myths and sagas which were still being transmitted freely throughout the island. These legends have provided scholars with an invaluable store of information about the ancient ways of the Celts.

Inevitably there has been much speculation about the extent to which Irish beliefs mirrored those on the continent. Here, some points of comparison are immediately evident. Both in Europe and in Ireland, Celtic religion focused heavily on nature. Water, in particular, seems to have been viewed with great reverence – sacred sites having been detected at such places as rivers, marshes, lakes, springs and wells. Their importance can be confirmed from linguistic sources, as well as archaeological finds.

Water Deities

The linguistic evidence can be gleaned from the number of European lakes and rivers that owe their names to Celtic deities. The Seine, for example, is called after the goddess Sequana. A surviving statuette indicates that she was visualized as a draped deity, riding in a duck-shaped boat. In general, water was revered for its life-giving qualities, but some gods had more specific associations. At the source of the Seine a healing shrine, dedicated to Sequana, was established during the Iron Age. Here,

pilgrims would cast tiny wooden images representing their ailments – an eye, a hand, a leg – into the waters, in the hope that the goddess would effect a cure.

In Ireland, both the Boyne and the Shannon were linked with female deities. The latter takes its name from a water spirit named Sinnan, while the Boyne is called after Bóann, a very similar figure. Bóann plays a greater part in Irish legend, through her adulterous mating with the Dagda (the father of the gods), which results in the

BOYNE VALLEY, COUNTY MEATH
This region featured prominently in ancient myth. It takes its name from Bóann, a powerful river-goddess who mated with the Dagda. His stronghold was at Brug na Bóinne, which is now identified with Newgrange.

birth of Oenghus, the god of love. The myths surrounding the origins of the two rivers are virtually identical. Bóann went in search of the Well of Segais, a fabulous spring in the Land of Promise, which was deemed to be the source of all knowledge. Nine hazel trees encircled the well and, when their nuts fell into the water, they created the *bolg fis* ('bubbles of inspiration'). These bubbles were swallowed by the Salmon of Knowledge, which transported the 'ideas' into Ireland's waters. The number of spots on the creature's back was said to equate with the number of nuggets of information that it had consumed.

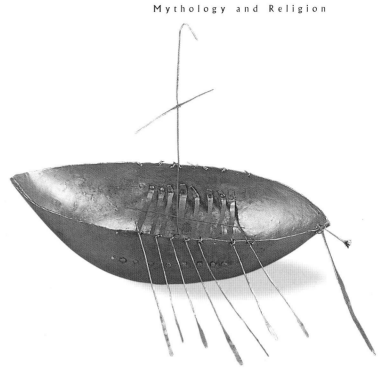

GOLD BOAT
This tiny model of a boat was among the objects discovered in the Broighter Hoard. It may have been meant as a tribute to the sea-god, Manannán mac Lir.

The well was protected by a taboo which barred all but a chosen few from looking on its waters. Bóann was not among this number, but she ignored the warning and strode contemptuously around the well, circling it four times. As she did so, the waters surged up, overspilled and drowned her. The path taken by the flooding waters duly formed the course of the River Boyne. There were deemed to be similar wells at the source of all Irish rivers (Sinann, for example, visited the Well of Connla). The ritual importance of hazelnuts dates back to Neolithic times, when they were placed in burial mounds and pits.

Throughout the Celtic world worshippers would seek to win the favour of water deities by offering up sacrifices to them. These took the form of precious objects – frequently high-quality arms and armour – which were cast away into the watery shrine. The most famous of these sacred sites was at La Tène, in Switzerland (see p.25), where two timber causeways were built at the edge of a lake. These allowed supplicants to walk out across the waters, before depositing their offerings in a suitable part of the lake. The object did not have to be fully submerged, however. In some areas they were simply placed on a marshy or boggy site. The owner of one of the most lavish Celtic objects, the Gundestrup cauldron, left it in plain view on a Danish peatbog, secure in the knowledge that no believer would be foolhardy enough to risk stealing it. Votive offerings of this kind have provided archaeologists in Ireland with some of their most valuable finds. Swords and scabbards have been dredged up from both the River Bann and the River Shannon, and it is feasible that the wonderful objects discovered at Lisnacrogher (see pp.58–60) were also intended as a sacrifice.

Shape-Shifting

The Celts' interest in nature worship extended to animals, and throughout the Celtic world a wide variety of animal sacrifices took place. These might simply have reflected a desire to offer up a worthwhile sacrifice – in pastoral communities such creatures were always a valuable

THE BROIGHTER HOARD

In 1896 ploughmen uncovered a group of golden objects near the shores of Lough Foyle. The finds included a bowl, two torcs, two wire bracelets and, most spectacular of all, a large, ornamental collar and a tiny model of a boat. These items date back to the first century BC and are thought to have been offerings to the sea-god, Manannán mac Lir.

The links with this marine deity were suggested partly by the find-spot – a salt-marsh, a typical site for offerings of this kind – and partly by the nature of the decoration. The collar is adorned with elaborate S-shaped motifs, often interpreted as sea horses, while the nautical connection is further emphasized by the boat. In 1903 the hoard became the subject of a legal dispute between the British Museum and the Royal Irish Academy. This revolved around the question of whether votive offerings were covered by the standard 'Treasure Trove' regulations, since the original owners had never intended to retrieve the objects. The Academy won the case and the hoard is now in the National Museum of Ireland in Dublin.

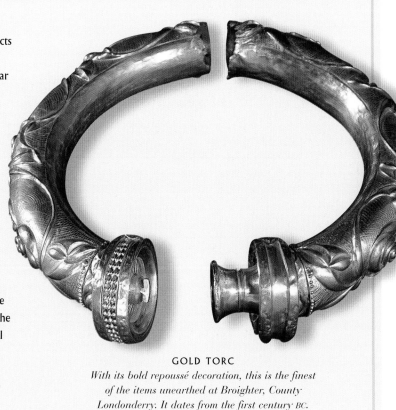

GOLD TORC
With its bold repoussé decoration, this is the finest of the items unearthed at Broighter, County Londonderry. It dates from the first century BC.

commodity – but the animal overtones of some deities suggest a deeper significance. In Ireland the fearsome war-goddess known as the Morrigán was closely associated with crows and ravens, while on the continent Cernunnos, a horned god of fertility, was linked to the stag, and Epona was a horse-goddess.

In other parts of the world, such as Egypt and India, animal gods were visualized as human figures with the head of a beast. Among the Celts, however, the gods were invariably conceived as humans, although they had the power to shape-shift at will into a creature. In so doing they sometimes displayed an ability to change into a succession of different forms. When the Morrigán challenged Cú Chulainn, for example, she assumed the guises of a black eel, a grey wolf and a hornless heifer.

The Cult of the Head

Another factor that links the Irish Celts with their continental cousins was a taste for offerings of a more grisly nature. Classical authors were both fascinated and appalled by their gruesome attachment to the practice of head-hunting. The Greek geographer Strabo was one of several commentators who noted the details:

The northern peoples display a trait of savage barbarity. When they ride away from the battlefield, they fasten the heads of their enemies to the necks of their horses. On returning home, they nail up this spectacle at the entrance to their homes. Posidonius [a historian and philosopher based in Rhodes, c. 135–c. 50 BC] says that he witnessed this sight in many places and was initially disgusted by it, but afterwards, becoming accustomed to it, could bear it with equanimity.

The rationale behind this terrible act was an unshakeable conviction that the severed head was a source of both physical and spiritual power. Accordingly the removal of an enemy's head was thought to bring both strength and prestige to the victorious warrior who carried out the deed. Sometimes the trophy was placed in a shrine, where it became the focus of various rites. Traces of two Gaulish shrines have been found at Roquepertuse and Entremont, both situated in Provence in southern France. Here, rows of human skulls were displayed in niches, in

---

As he does battle with a warrior named Loch, Cú Chulainn is confronted by a more dangerous foe – the Morrigán, the shape-shifting goddess of war:

Then Cú Chulainn felt something tugging at his feet. A huge, black eel coiled three times around his ankle and sent him tumbling into the water… Swiftly, he clambered up, dashing the eel against a stone, so that its ribs were broken. The creature loosened its grip but, almost at once, it turned into a grey she-wolf and brought cattle stampeding against him. Undaunted, Cú Chulainn took out his sling and sent a sharp stone speeding into the eye of the wolf. It reeled back in pain, just as Loch's sword cut into the Ulsterman once again.

Now the Morrigán came at Cú Chulainn in her final form, a hornless red heifer hurtling towards him. But the Hound of Ulster [Cú Chulainn's nickname] aimed his sling once more, loosing a shot that broke the animal's legs beneath her. The Morrigán came at him no more…

THE CATTLE RAID OF COOLEY
from the Táin Bó Cuailgne

---

purpose-built porticoes. Some still contained fragments of the weapons that had killed them. Similarly, at several Celtic burial sites in Britain, there is evidence of ritual decapitation of the deceased. The reasons are unclear, although it has been suggested that it was designed to ease the passage of the dead into the Otherworld.

There are no comparable archaeological sites in Ireland, but the early literature offers ample proof that similar ideas were current there during the Iron Age. In the *Táin*, for example, Cú Chulainn habitually removed the heads of his defeated enemies, displaying the skulls in prominent locations in order to throw fear into the hearts of the Connacht army. For their part, his adversaries recognized that decapitation was an inevitable hazard of war. In one episode, a mortally wounded warrior begged Cú Chulainn to allow him to make his farewells to his family, promising to return so that the Ulster champion could claim his rightful prize and behead him.

Classical sources also recorded the Celtic belief that human skulls could contain magical properties when used as drinking vessels. The Roman historian Livy (59 BC–AD 17) described how the Boii, a Celtic tribe from northern Italy, scraped out the head of a vanquished Roman general, gilded it, then used it in their rites. Echoes of this practice can be found in a tale from the Ulster Cycle concerning the remains of Conall Cernach, one of Cú Chulainn's foster-brothers. His fellow countrymen were able to gain relief from a curse which had deprived them of all their strength by drinking milk out of their former comrade's skull.

Smiths and Craft-Gods

Another distinctive feature of all Celtic societies was the special – almost magical – status accorded to the smith. The most remarkable objects produced by La Tène craftsmen were made out of bronze, and the subtle transformations that they could achieve with their metal ores remained a constant source of wonder to contemporaries. So while some ancient civilizations paid smiths scant regard – in Egypt and Rome, for example, they were seen as little more than labourers – the Celts conferred a most exalted status upon them.

From early times smiths were honoured with elaborate burial rites and were classed among the *áes dana* ('men of art'). The members of this learned class – which also included people who were judges, poets and doctors – were granted certain privileges, such as the right to move freely between tribes.

The Celtic reverence for the smith is evident from the number of craft-gods who are known to have been worshipped. In Ireland these were headed by the triad Goibhniu, Luchta and Creidhne, who forged weapons for the deity Lugh and for the Tuatha Dé Danaan. Goibhniu, as the smith-god, was the most important of the trio, creating a range of magical blades and spear-points which always found their mark. Luchta, as the god of carpentry, produced the shafts for these weapons, while Creidhne

the Artificer devised their various metal trappings. These included rivets for the spears, as well as sword hilts and shield bosses.

In addition to his role as armourer of the gods, Goibhniu also held another important post: he hosted the *Fled Goibnenn*, the Otherworld feast. The participants at this supernatural event ate meat from an inexhaustible cauldron and drank a special kind of ale which rendered them immune to disease and death. In this capacity Goibhniu is classified as one of the Celtic healing deities.

There must have been a European equivalent to Goibhniu, but his name is not known. In this respect the sizeable body of early Irish literature has proved invaluable to scholars, preserving details of many gods from the Irish pantheon. Students of the continental Celts are less fortunate. Only a handful of deities' names have been preserved on inscriptions or in the writings of foreign authors, and unfortunately the sources in question usually translated the gods into their classical equivalents. Julius Caesar, for example, remarked that:

The god they worship most is Mercury... They see him as the inventor of all the arts, the guide of all their roads and journeys, and the god who has the greatest power for commerce and money-making. After Mercury, they worship Apollo, Mars, Jupiter and Minerva...

Lugh of the Shining Countenance

In this instance Mercury can almost certainly be identified with Lugh, whose cult seems to have extended over much of Europe, as is confirmed by the numerous place-names that owe their origins to him. These include Lyons (Lugdunum), Laon and Léon in France, Liegnitz in Silesia, Leiden in Holland, and Carlisle (Luguvallum) in Britain. Lugh also featured prominently in Irish legend,

THE PAPS OF ANU, COUNTY KERRY
The name stems from an ancient tradition which likened these hills to the breasts of the mother-goddess Anu, the ancestress of the Tuatha Dé Danaan.

above all as the father and protector of Cú Chulainn. This Irish connection appears to have been a comparatively late development, however, for several of the early tales report that he came from overseas. They also describe him as *scál balb* ('the stammering spirit' – probably a reference to his foreign tongue.

Lugh's identification with Mercury has been made on the basis of his traditional epithet, *Samildánach* ('possessing many arts'), which corresponds closely to Caesar's 'inventor of all the arts'. Their primary roles were not particularly similar (Lugh was never a messenger), but both extended their influence over a broad range of different fields. The Celtic deity appears to have originated as a sun-god, for he was frequently known as 'Lugh of the Shining Countenance'. In addition, he was sometimes portrayed in the early sagas as a fertility-god or a peerless warrior ('Lugh of the Long Arm'). As the latter, he may have been a source for the Arthurian figure of Sir Lancelot.

Lugh was the most widely revered of all the pan-Celtic deities, but there is one other who has a special relevance in Ireland. This is Brigit, a triune goddess of healing, fertility and smithcraft, who may be equated with the Roman goddess Minerva. Brigit was the daughter of the Dagda and the consort of Bres, a half-Fomorian ruler of the Tuatha Dé Danaan. It seems highly likely that Brigit is synonymous with the British goddess Brigantia and the Gaulish deity Brigantu. More importantly, she is also intimately connected with St Brigid of Kildare (d. 525). They have the same feast-day, and many of the more colourful stories associated with the saint were undoubtedly adapted from the lore of the pagan goddess.

The Tuatha Dé Danaan

Whether in Ireland or in mainland Europe, Celtic gods differed from the deities of most other areas in one vital respect. They were not regarded as the creators of humanity, but rather as its ancestors. In Ireland this ancestral race was known as the Tuatha Dé Danaan ('People of the Goddess Danu') and its fortunes were outlined in the pseudo-historical work the Book of Invasions. Descended from the mother goddess, Danu or Anu, who gave birth to the Dagda and may have inspired the name of the River Danube, the Tuatha Dé Danaan ruled over Ireland after displacing the Fir Bolg, before eventually being superseded by the Milesians or Gaels. They cannot

BRONZE HEAD OF ST BRIGID
St Brigid is the Christianized version of the Irish goddess Brigantia. She was linked to the festival of Imbolc, which took place on 1 February and celebrated fertility.

exactly be described as 'invaders', since they were supposedly borne to Ireland on a row of clouds. Once there, they founded their capital at Tara and ushered in a period of peace and prosperity.

The Tuatha Dé Danaan came equipped with a formidable array of magical talents. The most powerful of their leaders were the Dagda, the father of the gods, who was also a specialist in druid lore; Manannán mac Lir, the principal sea-god; Dian Cécht, the healer of the gods; and Oenghus, the divine patron of music, poetry and love.

For all their supernatural powers, however, the Tuatha Dé Danaan were eventually swept aside by a race of mortals, the Milesians. At this stage, a deal was struck: the Milesians took control of the human world, while the ancient gods retired underground, taking up residence in the *sídhe* ('fairy mounds') that were dotted around the Irish landscape. In many cases, these *sídhe* were actually the remains of the megalithic tombs that had been built in

IRISH GODS

Badb	Goddess of death and battles
Bóann	Water-goddess, associated with the River Boyne
Brigit	Goddess linked with healing, poetry and crafts; also a fire-goddess
Creidhne	The Artificer, who made metal trappings for weapons
Dagda	Father of the gods
Danu	Fertility-goddess
Donn	Ancestor deity and god of death
Goibhniu	Smith-god, famed for his magical weapons; also a healing deity
Luchta	God of carpentry
Lugh	Sun-god, the father of Cú Chulainn
Manannán mac Lir	Sea-god
Medb	Goddess of sovereignty
Morrigán	Goddess of war and death
Nemain	War-goddess, who inspired panic and battle-fury
Nuadu	Warrior-god who lost an arm in battle and had it replaced with an artificial, silver one
Oenghus	God of love; the son of the Dagda
Tuatha Dé Danaan	General name for the ancient Irish gods

JANUS FIGURE, BOA ISLAND, COUNTY FERMANAGH

Taking its name from the goddess Badb, Boa Island was an important druidic centre. This sinister carving dates from the Christian era, but its inspiration is thoroughly pagan.

FOLLOWING PAGE – DOLMEN, POULNABRONE, COUNTY CLARE

Superstitious souls once believed that dolmens were giant altars where druid priests carried out human sacrifices.

pre-Celtic times. Even in their ruinous state, they were still sufficiently impressive to convince the Celts that they had been built by a superior, ancestral race.

Although defeated, the Tuatha Dé Danaan continued to enjoy a sumptuous lifestyle. Their subterranean *sídhe* were considered to be lavish palaces where the gods could indulge in endless feasting. Almost all the major prehistoric tombs were viewed in this way, along with some of the more striking natural features in the landscape. Among the better-known examples are Newgrange (see p.18), which became the dwelling place of the Dagda; Brí Léith (Ardagh Hill, County Longford), which was home to Midir, a chieftain of the Tuatha Dé Danaan; and Almu (the Hill of Allen, County Kildare), which was initially held by Nuadu and later passed to Fionn mac Cumhaill. As a result of this new arrangement, the Tuatha Dé Danaan acquired their alternative name, the *áes sídhe* ('people of the fairy mounds').

Gods or Superhuman Mortals?

Significantly, the gods still involved themselves in the affairs of mortals. They had the power of *féth fiada* ('lordly mist') – an ability to render themselves invisible, whenever they wished to roam on the surface world. They made use of this most frequently during the festival of Samhain (see p.82), when the barriers between the real and invisible worlds were temporarily laid aside. Even so, they could only influence, rather than control, the fortunes of their descendants. For the gods, as represented in the early sagas, were only semi-divine. This is particularly evident in the stories from the Ulster Cycle, where the distinction between god and mortal is far from clear. Many of the principal characters were clearly euhemerized deities whose divine powers had been downgraded to heroism or superhuman strength.

In some instances, this change of status can be confirmed from other sources. In the *Táin*, for example, Medb is portrayed as a human queen of Connacht. Only the squirrel and bird that perch on her shoulders offer a hint of her former shape-shifting powers. From a number of other independent tales, however, it is clear that Medb had previously been revered as one of the most important Irish deities. She was a goddess of sovereignty, a role that linked her closely with the initiation rites of the high king at Tara. In addition, she was worshipped as a goddess of both territory and fertility.

Several of the warrior-heroes in the *Táin* may well have had similar origins, although there is no firm evidence of cults relating to them. Cú Chulainn, Conchobar and Fergus all possessed magical weapons, which set them apart from ordinary men. In Cú Chulainn's case, the argument is even stronger, since there are several references within the epic to his divine parentage. When he is badly injured during the fighting, for example, his father (the sun-god Lugh) materializes out of nowhere, in order to lend assistance. This is not an isolated case of divine intervention, for the viewpoint in the *Táin* is complicated by the presence of a number of active deities. The most notable of these was the Morrígán, the awesome goddess of war, who confronted Cú Chulainn on a number of occasions.

For modern scholars the dwindling powers of the Celtic gods, as represented in the Ulster Cycle, had at least one beneficial side-effect. It meant that Christian monks were not deterred from copying down the early myths and legends, regarding them as colourful stories rather than as storehouses of pagan doctrine. The same cannot be said for the Celts' religious practices. With the exception of a few references to the sacred rites of kingship, virtually no details have been preserved in early Irish texts. Instead, once again, the most detailed information is found in classical sources.

The Priestly Caste

Greek and Roman commentators wrote at length about the priest-class, which administered religious affairs in the Celtic world. Much of the material is contradictory but, on the whole, they noted three distinct divisions within this special caste. These were the druids; the *vates* or seers; and the bards. Strabo, for example, reported:

> *Among the Gallic peoples, generally speaking, there are three kinds of men who are held in exceptional honour: the Bards, the Vates and the Druids. The Bards are singers and poets; the Vates, diviners and natural philosophers; while the Druids study both natural and moral philosophy.*

In Ireland, however, the position was slightly different. There, the seers were known by a different name – the *filidh*. As Christianity gained momentum, they became more important than their continental counterparts, gradually absorbing many of the duties of both the druids and the bards.

Nevertheless, during the heyday of the Celts the druids were clearly the most influential priestly body. The origin of their name is much disputed, although the most popular theory is that it was formed from a combination of the Greek word *dru* ('oak') and the Indo-European term *wid* ('to know'). Certainly, many Greek writers believed that the druids venerated oak trees. Pliny the Elder (AD 23/4–79), for example, stated that:

> *The druids consider nothing more sacred than mistletoe and the tree on which it grows, so long as it is an oak. They select oak groves for the sake of that particular tree, and will not perform any religious rites without its leaves.*

Modern authorities have cast doubt on this theory, however, believing that the reference to the oak was meant to signify all trees. They cite the close association between tree-lore and the ogham alphabet (see p.76), as well the linguistic similarity between the Irish words for knowledge (*fios*) and trees (*fid*).

The role of the druids has been the subject of much confusion, largely because of the highly coloured accounts that circulated during the Romantic era in the eighteenth and early nineteenth centuries. These fostered the notion that the druids were a bloodthirsty sect who presided over grisly human sacrifices in which the victims were burned alive in huge wickerwork images. They also perpetuated the myth that the druids were responsible for the creation of ancient megalithic monuments and stone circles, such as those at Stonehenge, Avebury and Carnac. Dolmens were habitually known as 'druids' tables', echoing the belief that the Celtic priests had used them as altars.

In fact, classical sources suggest that the original role of the druids was much more varied – if rather less dramatic than later accounts might imply. Their duties seem to have fallen into three main categories. First, they were the guardians of all tribal lore and knowledge, preserving it and passing it on to the next generation through a complex system of oral transmission. Second, they had to apply this knowledge in practical situations, acting as judges, royal advisers and arbitrators in disputes. Finally, it was their function to oversee the religious rites of the community. In the main, these seem to have focused on sacrifice and divination.

The most laborious aspect of the priestly role, and one that affected each of its three different classes, was learning the vast body of tribal knowledge. The druids opposed the use of the written word, wishing to restrict their learning to the holy men of the tribe. The only exception appears to have been the ogham inscriptions on memorial stones or boundary markers.

A Druid's Lot

Inevitably the training period was very lengthy. It has been estimated that it took a full twelve years to become accepted as a bard, and nineteen to reach the level of a druid. It is likely that druids also carried out some of the training for the bardic and *filidh* grades. The sacred texts and stories were learned by rote, probably using verse forms to assist the memory. A bard, for example, would begin as a 'Poet's Attendant' (*Tamhan*) and 'Apprentice Satirist' (*Drisac*), learning the ogham alphabet, the basics of grammar and twenty stories in his first year. During succeeding years he would memorize a prescribed number of poems, tales, orations and philosophy lessons. By his ninth year he would have become a 'Noble Stream' (*Anruth*), since 'a stream of pleasing praise issues from him, and a stream of wealth to him'. Finally, by the end of his training, his repertoire would include a staggering 350 stories. This number was confirmed in the Book of Leinster, which stated that any member of the *filidh* (who had by then taken over most bardic duties) ought to be able to recite 250 *príomscéalta* (main stories) and 100 *foscéalta* (secondary tales).

With all this learning at their command, it is not surprising that the druids and *filidh* were used as teachers. In his *De Bello Gallico*, Caesar noted the popularity of druid schools:

> *A great number of young men gather about them for the sake of instruction, holding them in great honour… Tempted by these great rewards [druids did not have to perform military service or pay tribute], many young men assemble of their own free will to receive their training, while others are sent by parents and relatives. Reports say that in the schools of the druids they learn by heart a great number of verses…*

Confirmation of this can be found in many of the early Irish legends, although the nature of these training centres varied considerably. In the tales about Cú Chulainn's boyhood, for example, the young warrior attends the classes of Cathbad, the chief druid of King Conchobar. Although mentioned only in passing, these classes appear to have been quite sizeable (one version of the text mentions that Cathbad had 100 pupils). By contrast, the schooling of Fionn mac Cumhaill was a much more intimate affair. He was taught by Finnegas the druid, who lived a solitary life by the banks of the Boyne. In this instance, the training was more akin to an apprenticeship: the youngster was taken into the druid's household in return for carrying out a number of domestic duties, such as cooking, for his master.

THE OGHAM ALPAHBET

Ogham is an ancient form of writing which flourished in Ireland from the fourth to the seventh centuries AD. It takes its name from Ogma, the Celtic god of eloquence and literature. Individual letters were formed from groups of straight or slanting lines carved on the edges of wooden staves or boulders. Most of the surviving examples are straightforward inscriptions, but the system was widely employed by the druids and was thought to have magical overtones.

The ogham alphabet may also have been linked to the druids' interest in tree lore. Each character is said to represent a different tree ('b' for 'birch', 'h' for 'hawthorn', and so on) and, more controversially, a different period in the calendar. According to this theory, the letter 'd' represented both the oak tree and the midsummer period of 10 June–7 July, the most sacred time in the druidic year. Similarly, the letter 'i' represented both the yew tree and the period around the festival of Samhain, at the start of November. Here again the yew tree, which symbolizes death and rebirth, was deemed a fitting emblem for Samhain's association with death and change.

LETTER	IRISH NAME	TREE
B	beith	birch
L	luis	rowan
F	fearn	alder
S	saille	willow
N	nuinn	ash
H	huathe	hawthorn
D	duir	oak
T	tinne	holly
C	coll	hazel
Q	quert	apple
M	muinn	vine
G	gort	ivy
NG	ngetal	broom/fern
STR	straif	blackthorn
R	ruis	elder
A	ailm	fir/pine
O	onn	gorse
U	ur	heather
E	edhadh	aspen
I	ido	yew
EA	ebhadh	aspen
OI	oir	spindle
UI	uileand	honeysuckle
IO	iphin	gooseberry
AE	phagos	beech

OGHAM INSCRIPTION, COLAISTE IDE, COUNTY KERRY
The invention of ogham is attributed to Ogma Cermait (Ogma the Honey-Mouthed), an Irish orator-warrior. Ogham stones are most common in County Kerry, but they are sometimes found outside Ireland, in Pictish areas of Scotland.

FOLLOWING PAGE – BEN BULBEN, COUNTY SLIGO
Sometimes written Beann Ghulban, this mysterious place is thought to owe its name to Conall Gulban, a son of Niall of the Nine Hostages.

Druids as Advisers and Arbitrators

The most respected druids also exerted a strong secular influence, acting as advisers to chieftains and kings. In a few early sources it is even claimed that some druids became kings themselves. Either way, their influence was considerable. In the stories from the Ulster Cycle, for example, Conchobar's druids were treated with such reverence that no one was allowed to speak before them or interrupt them. One unfortunate messenger who broke this rule paid for the offence with his life. In other texts druids attained positions of such importance that their identities were immortalized as place-names. According to the Book of Invasions, for instance, the kingdom of Meath was called after Mide, the chief druid of the Nemedians. After they had conquered Ireland, he lit a ritual fire at Uisnech, which burned continuously for seven years. As a reward, he was allowed to exact a tribute of a pig and a sack of grain from every Irish household. Another source told of an infamous druidess named Dub, who was drowned near the mouth of the Liffey, at a spot where the city of Dublin would later be built (from *Dubh Linn*, 'Black Pool').

The druids' role as judge and arbitrator is recorded in a number of classical texts. In his *Geographica*, Strabo explained that:

The Druids are considered the most just of men, and for this reason they are entrusted with the judgment, not only of private disputes, but also of public disputes; so that, in former times, they even arbitrated cases of war, forcing opponents to draw apart, when they were about to line up for battle.

Caesar expanded on this role in *De Bello Gallico*:

It is they who pass judgment in almost all disputes, public and private; and if any crime has been committed, or murder done, or if there is any dispute over succession or boundaries, it is they who decide it, apportioning both rewards and penalties. And if any man does not abide by their judgment, he is excluded from the public sacrifices, which is their heaviest penalty.

The final comment from this passage, which confirms that ostracism was deemed by the whole tribe to be far more serious than any physical punishment, tallies closely with some strictures from the Brehon Laws. These record that some of the most grievous crimes, such as murder or incest, were punishable by a form of banishment, in which the condemned person was set adrift in a coracle with no means of propelling it. Details of this kind lend weight to the theory that the Brehon Laws, which were eventually written down in the early medieval period, evolved out of druidic law.

Sacred Rites and Human Sacrifice

The final element of the druids' role – their supervision of religious ritual – was undoubtedly the most important aspect of their work, even if our knowledge of it is extremely limited. Where their ceremonies were concerned, the druids maintained great secrecy, and only one substantial description of a specific ritual is known to have survived. This is a passage in Pliny's *Natural History* of AD 77, giving details of a fertility rite. First, the druids gathered mistletoe, taking care to collect it on the sixth day of the moon (the first day of their month):

Below the tree, they prepare a sacrifice and a sacred feast, bringing two white bulls whose horns are tied for the first time. A priest clad in white climbs the tree, cuts the mistletoe with a golden sickle and catches it on a white cloth. Sacrifices are then made to the gods, to encourage them to look favourably on the offerings. They believe that mistletoe in a drink confers fertility upon any sterile animal and is a cure-all for any poison.

The question of human sacrifice has proved to be one of the most controversial areas of druidic activity. Many classical authors reported that the Celtic priests participated in these gruesome offerings, even if they did not actually carry out the killing. The druids' chief function, it seems, was to use the occasions for divinatory purposes. Both Strabo and the historian Diodorus Siculus (fl. first century BC) described how victims were stabbed in the back, so that the druids could make their prophecies by observing the death throes. In contrast, the Roman historian Tacitus (AD 56/7–after 117) reported that 'they deemed it a duty to cover their altars with the blood of captives, in order to consult their deities through observations of human entrails'. Irrespective of the method used for divining, most classical authorities agreed that the sacrifices were plentiful. The Roman poet Lucan (AD 39–65) told of 'altars piled high with hideous offerings', and of woods 'where every tree was drenched with human blood'. In spite of such accounts, there is comparatively little archaeological evidence. In Britain and Germany traces of human tissue and blood have been found next to stakes in ritual pits, but there is little to suggest that these practices were carried out in Ireland. The subject of human sacrifice is also noticeably absent from the principal myth cycles.

The Afterlife

The other aspect of druidic teaching that fascinated classical commentators was its notion of the afterlife. Citing a lost text by the Greek philosopher Posidonius (c. 135–c. 50 BC), Diodorus Siculus described the Celtic belief that 'the souls of men are immortal, and that after a certain number of years they live a second life, when the soul passes to another body'. Classical authorities became convinced that this theory was correct – partly because of the lavish grave-goods placed in Celtic tombs, and partly because of the reckless bravery that their warriors displayed on the battlefield, suggesting that death held no terror for them. The concept was also confirmed by numerous references in early Irish literature. Many stories told how the dead lived on in Otherworld *bruidhen* or 'hostels', feasting and drinking for years on end. There were also numerous references to regeneration. Dead warriors were brought back to life after being soaked in a magical cauldron or similar vessel. In the tale of *Cath Maige Tuired* (The Battle of Mag Tuired), for example, Dian Cécht, the physician of the gods, managed to restore to life many members of the Tuatha Dé Danaan by placing them in his healing spring. This worked on all warriors, save those who had been beheaded.

While most commentaries on the druids emphasized their barbarity, there was also acknowledgment of their scientific skill. Authors such as Caesar noted that they had 'much understanding of the stars and their motion, of the size of the world, of natural philosophy'. Such knowledge helped the druids to calculate time with considerable accuracy – a necessity, if they were to carry out their rites at the most auspicious times of the year.

The Coligny Calendar

The Celts used the moon as the basis of their measurements. They counted in nights rather than days, and calculated the start of individual months from the full moon, dividing them into half-months, rather than weeks. Any 'extra' days were accumulated to form an intercalary month, which was inserted whenever the need arose. Much of this information was confirmed by a unique druid artefact, the so-called Coligny Calendar (first century BC–first century AD). This consisted of a large bronze tablet, made in Gaul, showing details of sixty-two consecutive months and two intercalary months. One of its most intriguing features is the identification of lucky and unlucky times of the month, shown by the addition of the words *mat* (good) and *anm* (not good). No other calendar of this kind has come to light, but the ancient Irish legends contain many instances of druids making use of their divinatory powers. In the Ulster Cycle, for instance, Cú Chulainn took up arms at a very early age, after Cathbad the druid had named a specific date that was particularly suitable for the development of an outstanding warrior. Similarly, Queen Medb delayed the start of her campaign against Ulster by a half-month, after her druid had declared that the omens were unfavourable.

The druids also needed their skills in astronomy to help them calculate the major festivals of the year. They followed the so-called Eightfold Scheme, through which the year was divided up by eight significant dates: four of them with solar associations and four with lunar connections. The solar festivals are still very familiar today, consisting of the summer solstice – the date that is most visibly celebrated by modern-day druids; the winter solstice, which marks the apparent death of the sun; and the spring and autumn equinoxes. The four lunar festivals are linked more specifically with the Celts. They comprise Samhain (1 November, dark moon), Imbolc (2 February, new moon), Beltane (1 May, full moon) and Lughnasadh (1 August, old moon).

Celtic Festivals

On one level, Celtic festivals reflected different stages in the pastoral cycle. Samhain coincided with the slaughter of surplus cattle, which were then salted and stored away; Imbolc marked the height of the lambing season; Beltane was related both to mating time and to the purification of the herds; and Lughnasadh celebrated the harvesting of both human and animal fodder. Beyond this, however, each festival conjured up its own specific, highly individual set of associations.

Samhain was the most important of the festivals, coinciding with the Celtic New Year. Old fires were extinguished and had to be re-lit from a sacred flame, and each of the five kingdoms sent assemblies to a grand *feis* (a kind of fair) at Tara. More importantly, it was a time when the Celts remembered their dead ancestors, looking to them for guidance and inspiration. They could also make physical contact with them, for at Samhain the barriers between the real world and the Otherworld were lowered. This enabled the spirits of the dead to return to their former homes, to warm themselves by the hearth or even to commit some sinister act of mischief or revenge. Echoes of these various elements can be detected in the modern celebrations of Hallowe'en and All Saints' Day.

Imbolc was linked with fertility, since it marked the end of winter and the first glimmerings of spring. It was also associated with the healing- and fire-goddess Brigit and, through her, with St Brigid of Kildare. Beltane was a fire festival, probably named after the sun-god Belenus. It ushered in the summer and was commemorated with huge bonfires, which were erected on prominent hilltops. Lughnasadh was named after the sun-god Lugh and celebrated the gathering in of the harvest. It was a popular time for attending fairs, going horse-racing and arranging contracts of all kinds. Marriages that took place on Lughnasadh could be annulled a year later, upon the request of either party. In some areas the waning of the year was symbolized by a huge wheel which was set ablaze and then rolled down a steep hill.

The festivals proved to be the most enduring aspect of Celtic religion. In many parts of Ireland, they were still observed long after the coming of Christianity, even though the Church did its utmost to replace them with more appropriate forms of celebration.

KNOWTH WITH SATELLITE TOMBS, COUNTY MEATH

During the Celtic era prehistoric burial mounds were often described as sídhe ('fairy mounds') and were thought to be the dwelling places of the ancient gods.

CHAPTER FIVE

THE EARLY HISTORICAL PERIOD

In around the fifth century AD Ireland
began to emerge from the shadowy
realms of myth and legend. For the first
time the high kings at Tara and the
ruling dynasties, such as the dominant
Uí Néill, can be recognized as genuine
historical figures. The dates of their
reigns and the battles that they fought
can be verified from reliable sources.
During the same period missionaries
were busy converting the country to
Christianity, although it was a slow
process, and high kings such as Diarmait
probably only paid lip-service to the
new religion. Indeed, for many years
pagan and Christian traditions
flourished side by side.

COMERAGH MOUNTAINS, COUNTY WATERFORD
*Rising above Clonmel and the Suir valley, the Comeragh
Mountains lie just a few kilometres away from the coastline where,
according to some sources, the mythical queen Cesair
landed with the first Irish settlers.*

THE EARLY HISTORICAL PERIOD

The Recording of History

THE DIVIDING LINE BETWEEN history and prehistory is normally gauged by the existence of reliable historical records. In Ireland's case, this creates certain problems. There is a wealth of 'historical' information, extending far back into the early Celtic period – much of it very precise, giving the dates of battles and kings' reigns. However, it was actually written down long after the event and its accuracy is highly suspect.

In the first place, such records would inevitably have been prey to the distortions that naturally occur during long periods of oral transmission. Problems of this kind were exacerbated by profound changes in the Irish language which began to take effect in the fourth century AD. These alterations included lenition (the weakening of consonant sounds), the elimination of some syllables and the reduction of unstressed long vowels. As a result, a fourth-century name like 'Cunagusos' was replaced, over the course of the next century or so, by 'Congus'. Similarly, the word for poet was transformed from *velitas* to *file*. Such changes must have played havoc with the system of oral transmission, particularly since much of the material was passed down in verse form.

In addition there are concerns about the function of much of the material. Ancestry was extremely important to the Celts, and many individual tribes compiled their own king-lists, genealogies or annals. These were meant to illustrate the antiquity of the tribe, its line of descent from great figures – sometimes even gods or mythical heroes – and the importance of its past deeds. As a result, it is frequently impossible to tell whether these records preserve a genuine folk memory of distant events and people or are simply inventions, designed to give credibility to a later regime. On many occasions both elements may have been combined, with actual historical figures linked to 'facts' and dates that are later inventions.

The situation began to change around the fifth century AD, when Irish records can be confirmed from other sources. This is most apparent in matters relating to the spread of Christianity, where there are reliable Church records. In 431 a papal mission was sent to Ireland, headed by a bishop named Palladius. This was followed, later in the century, by the arrival of St Patrick, who founded his religious centre at Armagh. In the secular sphere the uncertainty continues for a little longer, although the broad shape of events becomes much clearer.

The Dominance of the Uí Néill

The first major trend concerns the emergence of the Uí Néill dynasty, who were to dominate Irish politics until the rise of Brian Boru in the eleventh century. The northern branch of the family was responsible for the break-up of the Ulster *cóiced*, as it was portrayed in the ancient sagas, while the southern Uí Néill seized Tara and proclaimed themselves high kings of Ireland.

In Ulster, the expansion of the Uí Néill was principally achieved at the expense of the Ulaid. Their capital, Emain Macha (see pp.38, 39), fell in the mid-fifth century and they retired eastwards. They continued to make claims to the overlordship of Ulster, but these were rarely realistic. One reason for their weakness, perhaps, was the absence of a strong, enduring dynasty, such as the Uí Néill. Instead, the kingship of the Ulaid changed hands frequently, usually passing to a member of the Dál Fiatach of eastern Down, the Dál nAraidi of Antrim or the Uí Echach Cobo of western Down.

Traditionally, leadership of the overcrowded province fell to the chieftain of the Dál Fiatach. Of the sixty-two rulers specified in the king-lists of Ulster, all but ten came from this family: the earliest chief who can be identified

NAVAN FORT, COUNTY ARMAGH
The Bronze Age hill-fort on this site is traditionally linked with Emain Macha, the royal seat of King Conchobar in the tales from the Ulster Cycle.

with any confidence is Muiredach Muinderg, who is thought to have lived in the late fifth century. He remains a shadowy figure, but one of his descendants achieved genuine prominence in the area. This was Báetán mac Cairrell, who ruled from 572 to 581. Despite the brevity of his reign, he appears to have achieved considerable status, although later annalists overstated the case, claiming that he was king of Ireland and Scotland, and that he received tribute from Connacht, Munster, Skye and the Isle of Man. Nevertheless, his fortress at Knocklayd, near Ballycastle, does seem to have been the focus of significant power.

Realistic assessments of Báetán's career suggest that he did manage to exert some control over the Isle of Man and the kingdom of Dalriada in Scotland. He led an expedition to the Isle of Man in 577, when he is said to have 'cleared' the place. This may mean that he expelled the Conailli Muirtheimne, an Irish tribe from south Down, substituting the rule of his own people. The presence of the Conailli Muirtheimne on the Isle of Man is confirmed by a contemporary ogham inscription. Báetán's success appears to have been short-lived, however, for two years after his death the Irish were driven off the island by the Dál Riata.

The Dál Riata Dynasty

Báetán's links with Man and northern Britain can be interpreted as evidence of his determination to offset the dominance of the Uí Néill by expanding overseas. This process had already been started by the Dál Riata, another of the beleaguered peoples living in Ulaid territory.

A truly pioneering dynasty, the Dál Riata traced their line back to Fergus mac Erc – sometimes known simply as Fergus Mór ('Fergus the Great'). In c. 500 he led an expedition of his people across the sea, to found a new settlement on the western coast of Scotland. The community chose Dunadd in Argyllshire as its stronghold, and in due course this became the capital of the Scottish kingdom of Dál Riata (or, more commonly, Dalriada). According to tradition, Fergus asked his brother, Muirchertach mac Erc, to help legitimize his new regime by sending across the *Lia Fáil*, the so-called Stone of Destiny, which played an important part in Ireland's royal ceremonies. Muirchertach did so, but – so the legend goes – Fergus neglected to return the precious item and it thus became the coronation stone of the future kings of Scotland (gaining renown as the Stone of Scone).

Fergus' original expedition was not an invasion, for it served the interests of other powers in the region and may well have been undertaken at their request. In particular, it was welcomed by the British kingdom of Strathclyde, since it provided a useful buffer zone against a growing threat from the Picts. Whatever the initial aims may have been, however, the colony soon prospered. Under the guidance of Fergus' descendants, Dalriada expanded to form the nucleus of the future kingdom of Scotland.

The Irish Dál Riata, meanwhile, did not abandon their homeland. For more than a century the Ulster and Argyllshire homelands remained part of the same kingdom, although inevitably this became the focus of disputes about the obligations of the Scottish Dál Riata. The Irish territories acknowledged the supremacy of the king of Ulaid, and attempts were made to extend this to the Scottish settlement. This appears to have been the chief subject under discussion at the Convention of Druim Cett (now Mullagh or Daisy Hill, County Londonderry), which was held in 575. Surviving accounts of this meeting of kings and clerics are very imperfect, but they do confirm that Dalriada was freed from its obligation to provide soldiers to the Irish high king, although the Scottish territory was still expected to lend assistance with its ships, should the need arise. The subtext of the agreement, however, was an alliance between the Uí Néill (the high kings at this stage) and the Dál Riata, to counter the threat of the powerful Báetán mac Cairrell. This alliance appears

CORMAC MAC AIRT

Cormac mac Airt was the most famous of early high kings of Ireland. Traditionally, he is said to have ruled at Tara from AD 227 until 266, but these dates cannot be substantiated and it is even possible that he was an entirely mythical character. Despite this, several tribes claimed descent from him – most notably the Uí Néill – and his name is commemorated in one of the ancient structures at Tara (Cormac's House).

Cormac's chief claim to fame stems from his links with Fionn mac Cumhaill and the Fianna. His reign coincided with their greatest exploits, and he was portrayed in the early literature as a kind of Irish King Arthur. He also played a leading role in some of the stories. In the *Echtrae Cormaic* (Adventure of Cormac), for example, he won a magical bough from the sea-god, Manannán mac Lir. The latter part of Cormac's career was rather less auspicious. He was forced to abdicate his throne after losing an eye in battle – thus infringing the rule that required high kings to have no physical blemishes – while his son, Cairbre, was responsible for the break-up of the Fianna.

to have held firm until the Battle of Mag Roth (Moyra, County Down) in 637, when the Uí Néill king, Domnall mac Aed, defeated a combined army of Cruthin and Dál Riata forces.

The Cruthin

The Cruthin, or *Cruithni*, were the other major force in Ulaid politics. Their name is the Q-Celtic version of the word Pritani, one of the most ancient races in Britain and Ireland. In the context of northern Britain, they are more familiarly known as the Picts, but this term was usually avoided in Ireland. The two divisions of the Cruthin people did not have close political ties and their social organization was significantly different. The Irish, for example, did not follow the Pictish custom of matrilinear descent (that is, royal succession through the female line). It has also been suggested that the word 'Cruthin' gradually became obsolete in Ireland during the eighth century, because it had unwelcome foreign overtones.

The chief dynasties of the Cruthin were the Dál nAraidi and the Uí Echach Cobo. The Dál nAraidi, based at Ráith Mór (County Antrim), appear to have been the dominant force, although it seems that for much of the

MOSAIC OF A CHARIOT RACE
The battle scenes described in the Táin *provide compelling evidence that the ancient Celts fought in chariots.*

time the Cruthin were a fairly disunited confederation of tribes. The Dál nAraidi claimed descent from Fiachu Araide, a semi-mythical figure who was said to have won a decisive victory against Cormac mac Airt, driving him out of Tara. In more historical terms, their most distinguished ruler was Congal Cloén (nicknamed Cáech, or 'the one-eyed').

Congal 'The One-Eyed'

Congal gained the kingship of the Ulaid in 627 and in the following year won a notable victory against an Uí Néill high king, Suibne Menn of the Cenél nEógain. In doing so, he may have been coming to the aid of another Uí Néill leader, Domnall mac Aed of the Cenél Conaill, who was reputed to have been his foster-father. Whether or not this is true, the pair soon fell out, for in 629 Domnall defeated Congal at the Battle of Dún Ceithirn (Duncairn, near Coleraine). This victory was not decisive, however, for Congal managed to orchestrate an alliance with the Dál Riata. His partner in this venture was the redoubtable Domnall Brecc. For a time they posed a genuine threat to Uí Néill supremacy, but this was eventually brushed aside on the battlefield of Mag Roth, where Congal lost his life.

Congal's period of influence was fairly limited, although he did briefly hold the post of high king. This nugget of information was preserved in – of all things – an ancient law tract on bee-keeping. Congal was partially blinded when a bee stung him in the eye, and he sought redress from the owner of the hive. The judgment was duly recorded in the tract, which described him as 'king of Tara, until the accident put him out of his sovereignty'.

Congal's achievements provided a rare interval in the long sequence of Uí Néill dominance. This status quo had been established in 563, when the northern Uí Néill inflicted a crushing defeat on an alliance of Cruthin tribes at the Battle of Móin Dairi Lothair. Seven Cruthin kings died on the field of battle, while according to St Columba's biographer, Adamnán (c. 625–704), an eighth, Eochaid Láeb, fled from the scene in his chariot. This tiny detail has attracted much attention from historians, since it suggests that chariots remained an essential part of Irish warfare right up until the dawn of the historical period, long after the heroic age described in the tales of Cú Chulainn.

The Cenél Conaill

The divisions of the northern Uí Néill are highly complex, although the two principal lines were probably the Cenél Conaill and the Cenél nEógain. The Cenél Conaill ('Kindred of Conall'), or Tir Conaill ('Land of Conall', later Tyrconnel), traced their line back to Conall Gulban, one of the sons of Niall Noígiallach. He established his kingdom in a region that included present-day County Donegal, together with large tracts of County Sligo. His descendants were to include several high kings, among them Báetán mac Ninnedo (d. 586), Máel Cobo (d. 615), Domnall mac Aed (d. 642) and Loingsech (d. 704).

Domnall and Loingsech appear to have been the most distinguished members of the family, being the only two to be hailed as 'kings of Ireland' in the *Annals of Ulster* – an important documentary source, which used such titles far more sparingly than most of its counterparts. Domnall certainly won a number of resounding victories over his rivals, but his name is most closely linked with the mythical tale of St Ruadan's curse on Tara (see pp.38–9), which caused him to establish a new capital at Dún na nGéd.

Little is known about Loingsech, other than that he reigned from 695 to 704, when he perished at the Battle of Corann (County Sligo). In any event, the fame of all these rulers was rapidly eclipsed by that of two Celtic saints – Columba and Adamnán – who were both members of the Cenél Conaill. Adamnán, in fact, was a fifth cousin of Loingsech.

The Cenél nEógain

The Cenél nEógain have become better known to posterity through their alternate name, Tir nEógain (Tyrone). The family traced its descent from Eógan, another of the sons of Niall Noígiallach. Eógan and two of his brothers (Conall Gulban and Enda) are sometimes equated with the Three Collas, who ransacked Emain Macha. Eógan

GRIANÁN OF AILEACH, COUNTY DONEGAL

Perched on its lofty site, the ring-fort was once as important as Tara or Cashel. The ancients believed that it was constructed by the Tuatha Dé Danaan.

also seized the fortress of Aileach, making it the centre of his new domains, which extended right across modern-day Tyrone, as well as parts of Derry and Donegal.

The Cenél nEógain could boast a long succession of high kings, beginning with the quasi-mythical Muirchertach mac Erc (d. 536). Little is known about him, apart from a string of (probably fictitious) battles and a strange tale about his supernatural death which related how he drowned in a vat of wine in the Otherworld. Muirchertach's sons, Forrgus and Domnall, appear to have ruled jointly as high kings at Tara, following their victory over Diarmaid mac Cerbaill at the Battle of Cúl Dreimne (561), but both of them died prematurely in 566.

Later incumbents included Aed Uaridnach (d. 612) and Suibne Menn (d. 628), who was deposed by Congal Cáech (628). However, the Cenél nEógain began to enjoy a greater period of influence in the eighth century, when their family rivals, the Cenél Conaill, began to decline. Loingsech's son was the last member of the latter to gain the kingship of Tara. After his defeat by Aed Allán of the Cenél nEógain in a crucial sea battle (734), the balance

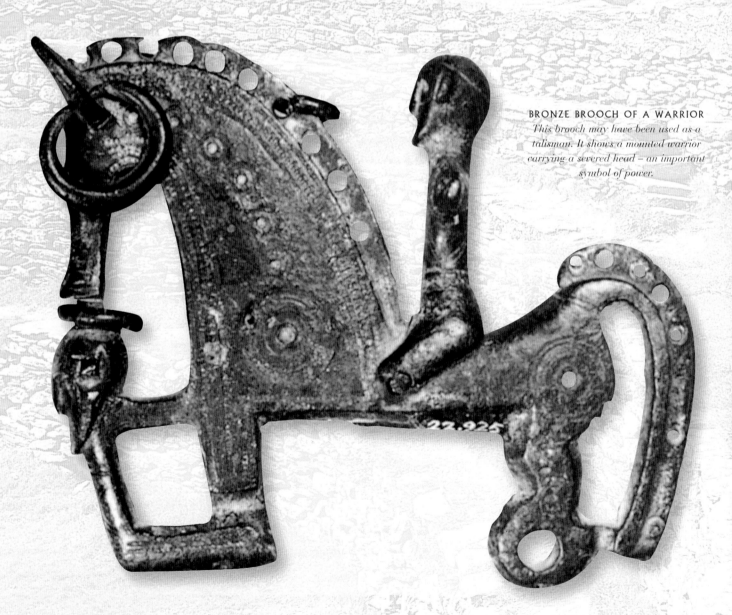

BRONZE BROOCH OF A WARRIOR
This brooch may have been used as a talisman. It shows a mounted warrior carrying a severed head – an important symbol of power.

GRIANÁN OF AILEACH, COUNTY DONEGAL
The literal meaning of grianán *is 'sun porch' or 'sunny place', but the thick, defensive walls of this fortress clearly demonstrate that its primary function was military.*

of power shifted. From that time on, the main contest for the high kingship was played out between the Clann Cholmáin ('Children of Colman') of the southern Uí Néill and the Cenél nEógain.

Following his convincing victory over the Ulaid at Fochairt (735), Aed Allán managed to secure the kingship, holding the crown from 736 to 743. During his reign, he subdued the Laigin, defeating them at the Battle of Áth Senaig (738, County Kildare), before meeting his end at the hands of Domnall Midi, who thereby became the first member of the Clann Cholmáin to attain the office of high king.

Just as the Cenél nEógain were the rising power in the north, so the predominance of the Clann Cholmáin was a new development in the central kingdom of Mide. The principal dynasties of the southern Uí Néill had long been the Síl nAedo Sláine ('the Seed of Aed of Slane') and the Clann Cholmáin, but it was the former who had generally maintained overall control. Of all the dynastic rivalries in Ireland, it was the struggles of the southern Uí Néill that carried the greatest significance. This was because their territory contained the sacred site of Tara, the traditional seat of the Irish high kings.

The High Kingship

The office of high king was enormously prestigious, but there are many puzzling features about the nature of the title. Not least of these was the role of Tara itself. Its prehistoric remains are very ancient, dating back to Neolithic times, even if the actual structures are nothing like as impressive as the megalithic monuments in the Boyne complex. Nevertheless, it clearly had immense ritual significance, and echoes of this survived well into the Middle Ages. Such ritual importance should not imply that Tara was a genuine capital, however, for there is no suggestion that medieval kings took up residence there. Quite the reverse; excavations have shown that the site of Tara was abandoned long before the early medieval period, at the very time when the office of high king was growing in importance.

Closely associated with this was the question of the high king's function. Even when the office was at the peak of its prestige, it remained fundamentally different from other Western kingships. It does not appear to have offered any significant economic, political or territorial advantages. The Uí Néill, for example, throughout their long tenure of the high kingship, did not exert any greater influence outside their traditional spheres of influence. Despite this, the ambition to secure the title was universal, as the concocted genealogies and king-lists of the provincial kingdoms demonstrate all too clearly.

The solutions to some of these mysteries can be found in the early legends. Many of these placed emphasis on the geographical importance of Tara. Its name in Irish is *Temair* (literally 'a place with a view') and, from its highest vantage point, it was possible to make out landmarks in each of the other *Cóiceda*. In this respect, it was similar to the Hill of Ushnagh, the so-called navel of Ireland,

which was also located in the Middle Kingdom. These two sites were invariably mentioned together, as the twin ritual centres of the country. It has even been suggested that they held a genuinely 'national' significance which was recognized throughout Ireland. This theory is based on Caesar's comments about regular gatherings of the druids in Gaul. He noted that their principal meetings always took place in the territory of the Carnutes, at the very heart of Gaul, and that their delegates came from all parts of the country. In a spiritual sense, therefore, the various Gallic tribes were united, even if in military and political affairs they were hopelessly divided. This offers a telling comparison with the situation in Ireland, where internal rivalries were manifold, but there was universal respect for the high kingship.

Early literature offers several hints that Tara was also one of the entrances to the Otherworld. In particular, it suggests that the profusion of forts and raths on the site

THE CAT STONE, COUNTY WESTMEATH
Lying near the Hill of Ushnagh, this huge boulder is often identified as the legendary Ail na Míreann ('Rock of the Divisions'), the so-called navel of Ireland.

CELTIC TABOOS

One of the most curious aspects of Celtic belief was the taboo, or *geis* (plural *gessa*), which placed constraints upon the actions of many leading figures in the early sagas. The fact that so many of these *gessa* were directed specifically against kings has given rise to the theory that the practice originated in early kingship rituals. Only a small minority of the gessa can now be interpreted satisfactorily. In Conaire Mór's case, for example, the proscription against hunting birds stemmed from the fact that his father was a bird-like deity, while the instructions about walking round Tara echoed ancient beliefs about the power of the sun. According to these, a person could ward off evil influences by taking a 'sunwise turn' (that is, walking in a path that followed the course of the sun). The remainder of Conaire's *gessa*, however, appear quite baffling (see p.96).

The *geis* originated in the prehistoric era and had definite magical overtones, but its influence lingered for many centuries. A typical example concerns the planetary system: the Celts were proficient astronomers, but the names of the individual planets were forbidden druidic words. Instead, people were expected to refer to them by means of euphemisms. Thus the moon was known by such terms as 'brightness', 'radiance' or 'queen of the night'. This proscription lasted into the Christian period and many Irish planetary names were thus lost, to be replaced by borrowings from other languages.

BRONZE FIGURE OF A BIRD
Birds were widely venerated in Celtic lands, where they were often linked with omens and prophecies. Some Irish gods also shape-shifted into birds in the course of their dealings with humanity.

was not designed to keep out mortal attackers, but to protect the outside world from the hostile forces that could pass through supernatural barriers during the festival of Samhain (see p.82). A typical story relates how Fionn mac Cumhaill won the friendship of Conn Cétchathach by rescuing Tara from the clutches of Aillén mac Midgna, a fire-breathing goblin who used to burn the place to the ground each Samhain. Similarly, Conn himself was bound by a strict *geis* (taboo), which required that he should patrol the ramparts of Tara every day, to prevent the fairy people of the *sídhe* from stealing out and taking control of Ireland once again.

The Feast of Tara

❧

The ancient legends have also preserved revealing details about some of the rites that surrounded the kingship of Tara. At the heart of the ceremonies was a ritual union between the mortal king and the goddess of sovereignty, who personified the land. In general, this rite was known as a *banais righe* ('wedding-feast of kingship'), although at Tara it was called a *feis temrach* ('feast of Tara'). The goddesses varied from place to place, but at Tara the key deity was Medb. In the stories from the Ulster Cycle she was portrayed as nothing more than a warrior-queen, albeit a very powerful one. A few passages from earlier tales, however, hint at her divine origins. In one of these she boasted that she had mated with no fewer than nine sacred kings, and that she would allow no mortal man to rule at Tara unless he had first coupled with her. This promiscuity offers convincing proof of Medb's divine function, for it confirms that she was involved in the initiation of each new king. Her very name provides further evidence of this: Medb means 'she who intoxicates' – an obvious reference to the libations of wine that formed part of the ceremony.

The ritual marriage of the king and goddess symbolized the crucial relationship that existed between the ruler and his land. For it was believed that the fertility and prosperity of the kingdom were intimately bound up with the actions and character of the high king. This did not simply entail bravery on the battlefield, or a sense of fair play when dispensing justice; it even extended to the ruler's physical appearance. He had to be free from all blemishes, or else he was required to abdicate. This point was illustrated in the tale of Nuadu, one of the kings of the Tuatha Dé Danaan. He led his people to a notable victory over the Fir Bolg at the Battle of Magh Tuiredh, but in the process his arm was severed by an enemy warrior, forcing him to renounce his crown. He managed to regain it at a later date, however, after Dian Cécht, the healing-god, had fashioned him a new arm made out of silver. This story dates from archaic times, but the strictures about physical perfection remained in force during the historical period. As we have seen, Congal Cáech lost his throne at Tara after a bee blinded him in one eye.

Conaire Mór has been confirmed as the high king of Tara, but only on condition that he obeys a number of stringent gessa, or taboos:

> *You are forbidden to cast at birds, for every bird is natural to you… You may not pass Tara on your right-hand side, or Brega on your left. You may not hunt the wild beasts of Cernae. You may not stay abroad from Tara for the space of nine nights. You may not spend the night in a house, where firelight is visible after sunset, from within or without… A company of one man or one woman may not enter your household after sunset. You may not intervene in a dispute between two of your servants.*

THE DESTRUCTION OF DA DERGA'S HOSTEL
from the Togail Bruidne dá Derga

DRINKING HORNS, SIXTH CENTURY
Many of the most sacred ceremonies involved libations to the gods. Linguistic evidence of this is supplied by the name of the goddess Medb. Its literal meaning is 'she who intoxicates', and it comes from the same root as 'mead'.

The ritual method of selecting a new king was described in the heroic tale of *Togail Bruidne dá Derga (The Destruction of Da Derga's Hostel)*. It involved a *tarbfheis* ('bull-feast'), in which a bull was slaughtered and a man was given its meat to eat and its broth to drink. He was then put to sleep, and 'an incantation of truth' was chanted over him by four druids. This, it was believed, would enable him to identify the next king in his dreams. Once selected, the prospective king still had to pass a number of rigorous texts: he had to be able to drive the royal chariot; he had to be the right size for the robes of state; and, most important of all, he had to place a hand on the *Lia Fáil*, the Stone of Destiny. According to tradition, this uttered a piercing scream whenever it was touched by the rightful king.

Myth or History?

Later annalists compiled lengthy lists of the high kings, beginning with Sláinge, who was said to said to have ruled in the twentieth century BC. Clearly, many of these lists were fanciful inventions, and it is hard to know where historical reality begins. The oldest of the surviving texts, the Baile Chuind (The Vision of Conn), was composed during the reign of Fínsnechta Fledach (675–95). It enumerates the successors of Conn Cétchathach, including several kings who, if nothing else, were regularly claimed as ancestor-figures by the principal Irish tribes. The most celebrated of these were Cormac mac Airt (see p.88) and Niall Noígiallach (see p.50), both of whom may have been historical figures, even though their lives are obscured by mythological associations. Cormac's memory was revered because his reign represented a golden age during which the adventures of the Fianna took place, while Niall gave his name to the powerful Uí Néill dynasty.

Some high kings were also mentioned in early Christian sources. Muirchú's *Life of St Patrick*, written in the seventh century, was one of a number of texts that described the saint's confrontation with Laoghaire, the son of Niall. Laoghaire's dates have been estimated as c. 427–c. 462, but the details of his clash with St Patrick are probably as fictitious as the legends surrounding his pagan ancestors.

ST PATRICK WITH AN IRISH KING
According to legend, St Patrick launched his ministry in spectacular fashion by converting the pagan king Laoghaire on the Hill of Slane.

The same is true of the next symbolic confrontation between the two cultures. This occurred in the sixth century, when St Ruadán is said to have placed a curse on Tara and its pagan rulers – a move that proved so effective that the king was converted to Christianity and Tara's heathen temples were abandoned. The story of the curse is undoubtedly apocryphal, and many scholars have queried whether St Ruadán himself ever existed. Instead, by a curious irony, the most accurate elements of the tale concern the recipient of the curse, Diarmait mac Cerbaill.

Diarmait – a Christian High King

Diarmait is probably the first of the high kings whose claim to genuine historical status is universally acknowledged. He is thought to have ruled c. 545–c. 65, and is recognized as the progenitor of both the Síl nAedo Sláine and the Clann Cholmáin tribes. He is also said to have been the last high king to participate in a *feis temrach*, although the reasons for this are disputed. Christian sources believe it was due to his conversion to Christianity, while others suspect he only paid lip-service to his new faith and the ceremony of the feast of Tara fell out of use in the chaos that followed Diarmait's rule.

Certainly, both Diarmait's reign and its aftermath were marked by almost continual warfare. In the years before 560 he had to contend with uprisings by the Laigin and the death in battle of one of his sons, Colmán Már, at the hands of the Cruthin (555 or 558). Subsequently, there was trouble from both the Ulaid and the northern Uí Néill. The latter inflicted a heavy defeat upon Diarmait at the Battle of Cúil Dreimne (561), a clash that is said to have been instigated by St Columba (c. 521–97?). Despite this setback, Diarmait remained in power for a further four years, before being slain during a foraging expedition.

In spite of Diarmait's considerable posthumous fame, he and his successors appear to have maintained an extremely tenuous hold on the kingship. Dynastic genealogies suggest that he was succeeded by his third son, Aed Sláine – the forefather of the Síl nAedo Sláine – but this is not confirmed in the *Baile Chuind* or in other independent sources. Indeed, virtually nothing is known about Aed, apart from the curious legend that his mother (the sovereignty goddess of Munster) had given birth to a trout. General recognition of the supremacy of the southern Uí Néill did not occur until the mid-seventh century, when two brothers, Blathmac and Diarmait, ruled jointly as high kings. Both were included in the *Baile Chuind*, even though their reign was comparatively brief. Diarmait achieved a notable victory against the northern Uí Néill, defeating and killing Conall Cáel, but both he and Blathmac perished in the terrible plague epidemic that swept across Ireland in 664–6.

Ironically, the plague enabled two of Blathmac's sons to maintain the family grip on the crown, as it wiped out their most dangerous rivals. Sechnussach ruled for six years (665–71), before losing his life in a quarrel with a king of the Cenél Cairpre. He was succeeded by his younger brother, Cenn Fáelad, who was killed at the

THE CULT OF THE HERO

The period that is captured so graphically in the tales of the Ulster Cycle is often described as the heroic age. This refers both to the nature of the characters themselves and to their attitudes towards warfare and honour. Many of the leading figures in the tales trod a fine line between weakened deities and superhuman mortals, although it obviously suited the Christian scribes, who were preserving the material, to portray them as the latter.

At the same time, many of the war like traits described in the *Táin* tally closely with the attitudes of the Iron Age Celts as described by classical authors. There is a love of proud boasts, of improbable challenges and of single combat. There is also an appreciation of fine weaponry and supreme martial skills. Cú Chulainn takes these qualities to the limit: he chooses a brief but glorious life, in place of longevity; takes to the battlefield at an impossibly young age; and confronts vast numbers of enemies single-handed. The emphasis, in short, is on the individual. By the time Fionn mac Cumhaill enters the scene the mood has changed. Heroism is still there in abundance, but it is now allied to a greater sense of teamwork. For all his fine qualities, Fionn is surrounded by warriors with even greater skills, and there are early hints of the Arthurian values that would dominate later Celtic tradition.

Battle of Aircheltra (675). Diarmait's descendants had to wait until the following century before gaining the throne. The successful incumbent was Fogartach, Diarmait's great-grandson. After a number of defeats early on in his career, one of which forced him to seek temporary refuge in Britain, he seized the vacant kingship in 722, but held office for just two years before falling in the Battle of Cenn Deilgden (724). After this, the Clann Cholmáin took over the mantle as the leading power among the southern Uí Néill.

GLENCOLUMBKILLE, COUNTY DONEGAL
This ancient cross-slab is one of the stations on a turas (pilgrimage) dedicated to St Columba (Colum Cille). Traditionally, the event is said to commemorate the saint's successful battle of wits against a demon.

The 'Children of Colman'

The Clann Cholmáin took their name from Colmán Már, the largely anonymous son of Diarmait mac Cerbaill, who had been slain by the Cruthin in 555 or 558. However, it was only with Domnall Midi that this tribe came to the fore. He ruled for twenty years (743–63), which was in itself an exceptional feat at the time, and his reign was remarkably peaceful. Domnall even managed to combine his temporal role with the call of his faith. On two occasions he briefly relinquished the reins of office and went into a monastic retreat.

Domnall's son, Donnchad Midi, was an equally dominant figure, but his lengthy reign witnessed a renewal of hostilities on virtually all fronts. Much of his time was spent in conflict with the south. In 770 he launched a punitive expedition into Leinster, to assert his suzerainty over the Laigin. Here, his particular aim was to quash any thoughts of rebellion from Cellach mac Dúnchada, who had recently won victories over local rivals. Donnchad did not seek to provoke a major battle. Instead, he camped for a week at the hill-fort of Dún Ailinne, sending out his warriors to lay waste to the surrounding countryside, before returning north. Five years later, Donnchad travelled south again, this time to do battle with the forces of Munster. Once again he was successful, defeating (among others) the soldiers mustered by the monastery of Durrow.

In the north Donnchad had to contend with Domnall, the ruler of Ailech, whom he defeated in 779, and with the descendants of Aed Sláine, who were subdued by royal victories at the Battles of Forcaladh (778) and Leafin (786). Donnchad remained in power until 797, when he was finally defeated and killed by Aed mac Néill, at the Battle of Drumree.

**ST KEVIN'S KITCHEN,
GLENDALOUGH, COUNTY WICKLOW**

The monastery at Glendalough was founded by St Kevin, a member of the ruling Leinster dynasty, who gave up his worldly position in order to become a hermit. Despite its curious name, this 'kitchen' was probably intended for use as an oratory or a mortuary chapel. Its nickname suggests that there may once have been a pagan hearth-stone on the site, which the monks adapted for Christian use.

The Leinstermen

Events in the southern half of the country are slightly less easy to follow, if only because the ruling factions played a smaller role in the disputes over the high kingship of Tara. In Leinster, the situation was further complicated by the fact that, prior to the eighth century, the principal sources of information were produced by the Uí Néill, who could hardly be described as neutral observers.

In the earliest, shadowy part of their history, the Leinstermen had extended their influence a long way north, holding sway over Tara and much of the Middle Kingdom. However, a string of defeats at the hands of the Uí Néill, culminating in the slaughter at Druim Derg (516), shifted the balance of power irrevocably. The territories in the Middle Kingdom were lost, and many of the tribes that had played an important part in the formation of the province now began to fade from view. These included the Uí Garrchon, the Uí Máil, the Uí Failgi (who gave their name to County Offaly) and the Dál Messin Corb. Instead, the early historical period was dominated by two main dynasties, the Uí Dúnlainge in the north and the Uí Cheinnselaig in the south.

These two peoples had close family connections. They both claimed descent from a common ancestor, Bresal Bélach (a mythical king of Tara), and their respective founders, Dúnlang and Enna Cennsalach, were reputedly first cousins. Enna's son, Crimthann (d. 483 or 486), was cited as the first member of his dynasty to become king of the Laigin, while the first of the Uí Dúnlainge to achieve this honour was Illann (d. 527). The historical accuracy of these chiefs and their dates, however, cannot be gauged with any certainty.

The first figure of any real prominence among the Uí Dúnlainge was Fáelán mac Colmáin. He won the kingship of the Laigin in 633, after defeating Crimthann of the Uí Máil at the Battle of Áth Goan. The annals record a number of victories in subsequent years, most notably in skirmishes with Crundmáel Bolg Luatha (the leader of an offshoot of the Uí Cheinnselaig), and in a pitched battle with the king of the Osraige. Even so, Fáelán's importance is more evident from Christian sources. These link him closely with St Kevin (d. c. 618), the founder of the influential monastery of Glendalough, in County Wicklow.

who was reputed to have been his foster-father. In addition to this, Fáelán's brother and nephew both became bishops of Kildare, the most prestigious ecclesiastical post in the region.

Among the Uí Cheinnselaig, the leading figure was probably Brandub mac Echach. He was accepted as over-king of the Laigin in 591, following the death of Aed Cerr. The reason for his selection may well have been the defeat that he had inflicted on the Uí Néill at Cloncurry the previous year. If so, then the Leinstermen were vindicated in their choice, for Brandub achieved an even more emphatic victory at the Battle of Dún Bolg in 598, when the high king, Aed mac Ainmerech, was slain. The background details of this conflict have survived only as a colourful legend which suggests that a serious slight was made against Brandub's wife. Whatever the cause of the dispute, the Laigin chief followed it up with a series of raids into the Middle Kingdom. Here, he appears to have won some territory from the Uí Néill, while a group of his immediate descendants, the Fir Thulach Mide, were granted a petty kingdom within the lands of the Clann Cholmáin. Brandub's demise was rather less glorious. He was killed in 605 by a fellow member of the Laigin, possibly his own son-in-law.

Men of Munster

The course of Munster's early history is even sketchier than that of Leinster. This is due to the political isolation of the *cóiced* and to the dearth of reliable records. There is a gap of some ninety years between the first available date (the death of Oengus in 490) and the second (the death of one of his descendants, Coirpre Cromm, in 579/80) and, of course, neither of these dates can be verified. It was once suggested that Munster was remarkably peaceful during the Dark Ages, but in truth this is probably an illusion. The endless lists of battles and skirmishes that fill the annals from other parts of Ireland are simply unknown. Genealogies do exist but, without the background dates, it is almost impossible to fit them into a proper chronological framework.

In general terms, the Eóganachta remained the dominant force in the region, although they branched off into a number of separate dynasties. The genealogies list seven main lines (the Eóganacht Chaisil, Aine, Locha Léin, Raithlind, Glendamnach, Arann and Ruis Argait), but historians have adjusted this slightly, most notably with the addition of the influential Eóganacht Airthir Chliach. The kingship of Cashel – the most important title in the south – rotated fairly regularly between these groups.

In the early historical era Munster's most fruitful period seems to have occurred during the sixth century. There was considerable expansion to the north, into the lower reaches of Connaught, the Burren region of County Clare and even on to the Aran islands. This trend was reversed in the eighth century, although the same period witnessed the rise of the most powerful of Munster's early kings. This was Cathal mac Finguine

KINGSTON BROOCH
Celtic artefacts such as this sixth/seventh-century brooch were noted for the maze-like intricacy of their design. Interlacing and knotwork were particularly popular motifs

(d. 742), who was a member of the Eóganacht Glendamnach. In alliance with a Laigin force, he led a raiding party into Uí Néill territory in the plain of Brega in 721. Subsequently, however, he broke with the Laigin, forming a pact in 737 with the new high king, Aed Allán mac Fergaile. It is quite possible that Cathal was nursing ambitions of becoming high king himself but, in the event, he died a year prior to his ally.

Despite Cathal's success, the inherent weakness of Munster's situation rapidly became apparent. The Eóganachta had never displayed the same cohesion as the Uí Néill, and this became a genuine prob-lem, as the *cóiced* gradu-ally began to split in two. Theoretically

CARPET-PAGE, *BOOK OF KELLS*
*Carpet-pages were ornamental sections
in early Celtic manuscripts, usually
based around the symbolism of the
Christian cross.*

at least Cashel retained the primacy of the whole region, but the divisions between the two sectors (later to become known as Thomond and Desmond) were obvious to everyone. In all likelihood, they may have encouraged Donnchad Midi of the Clann Cholmáin to launch his fero-cious attacks on Munster in 775/6.

By this stage, the impetus of Irish politics was already entering a new phase. In 797 Aed mac Néill of the Cenél nEógain wrested the throne from Donnchad Midi and seized it for himself. From this time on, he became better known by a new name, Aed Oirdnide ('the Ordained'). This unusual term has led historians to believe that his inauguration was governed by the Church. If so, then it marks the completion of the conversion process, and the ultimate recognition of Christianity's influence at the highest possible level of human affairs.

CHAPTER SIX

THE CHRISTIAN ACHIEVEMENT

Despite dramatic tales of St Patrick's achievements, it was probably not the saint himself, but a cleric called Palladius, who actually brought Christianity to Ireland. One of the most prominent of the many holy men to follow them was St Columba, who established a fellowship of monasteries throughout Ireland and beyond. Many Christian converts lived a solitary existence as hermits, celebrating the glories of nature and their beliefs in poetry and in the illuminated gospels for which they are now probably best remembered. The flowering of Celtic culture also produced elaborate box-shrines, decorated caskets for saintly relics, and monumental stone crosses.

CROSS-SLAB, THE SKELLIGS
Lying off the tip of County Kerry, the Skellig Islands became home to a group of early Christian anchorites.

THE CHRISTIAN ACHIEVEMENT

The Mission of Palladius

Contrary to popular belief, St Patrick was not responsible for introducing Christianity into Ireland. Instead, the earliest documentary evidence relates to the mission of a cleric named Palladius. In 431 Prosper of Aquitaine (c. 390–c. 463) noted in his *Chronicle*: 'To the Irish believing in Christ, Palladius, having been ordained by Pope Celestine, is sent as first bishop.' From this entry two things are apparent: first, that a Christian community already existed in Ireland; and, second, that it was deemed sufficiently important to merit the attention of a high-ranking official who had been personally ordained by the Pope himself.

Further information about Palladius and the fate of his mission is disappointingly vague. In all probability he can be identified with the Palladius who, in 429, had persuaded the Pope to send Germanus of Auxerre (c. 378–448) to Britain to root out a group of heretics; some scholars also believe that Palladius accompanied Germanus on this mission. But Palladius' own origins are obscure. It may be that he had trained under Germanus in Auxerre, although it is equally possible that he was either Roman or British.

After his arrival in Ireland, Palladius appears to have concentrated his efforts in the Wicklow region. He is cited as the founder of churches at Donard, Tigroney and

Killeen Cormac, although none of these associations can be proved, since no contemporary record of his mission has survived. Later commentators implied that his venture was a comparative failure, and that he soon left Ireland to preach in Scotland. This may be true – Palladius appears to have become the focus of a cult in the Aberdeen area – but the value of the later reports is certainly open to question. Most were written by churchmen who were keen to promote the role of St Patrick in order to confirm the primacy of Armagh, and it was naturally in their interests to minimize the contribution of his rivals.

No one knows precisely how Christianity reached Ireland, but the immediate source is likely to have been Britain. Some of Ireland's earliest Christian terms derived from British words, or from British versions of Latin (*Cáisc* for 'Easter', *cruimthir* for 'priest'). The initial converts may have been settlers, traders or even slaves. The case for the latter is strengthened by the fact that St Patrick himself was brought to Ireland as a captive.

St Patrick's Role

Both the life and the role of St Patrick have been the subject of much controversy. Historians are fortunate that some of his writings have survived – most notably his *Confession* and his *Letter to Coroticus* – since these provide a few kernels of biographical information. They indicate that his name was Patricius and that he came from well-born Romano-British stock. He grew up in *Bannavem Taburniae*, an unidentified location in western Britain, where his father, Calpurnius, was both a *decurio* (a civic official) and a deacon. Patrick was raised as a Christian but, at the age of sixteen, was captured by a raiding party and taken to Ireland as a slave. He remained there for the next six years, primarily tending the herds of his new master, and it was during this time that his faith deepened and he acquired his sense of vocation.

SAUL, COUNTY DOWN
This chapel was constructed on the site of 'Patrick's Barn', the first church to be founded by the saint.

The remainder of Patrick's career is less certain, since the surviving accounts have been heavily embellished by later commentators. Nevertheless it appears that, after regaining his liberty, Patrick rejoined his family in Britain and undertook a basic form of training for the ministry (he often bemoaned his lack of a 'higher education'). He also spent some time in Gaul, before embarking on his mission to Ireland. There he began preaching at Saul, County Down, before establishing a more permanent base at Armagh, which was later to claim primacy over the entire Irish Church.

The most contentious aspect of Patrick's career is the chronology. The saint's writings contain no clues concerning the exact dates of his life or of his mission in Ireland. Until recently, most authorities estimated that he lived from c. 390 to c. 460, based on the assumption that his expedition took place shortly after that of Palladius, perhaps in c. 432. Increasingly, however, opinion has shifted towards a slightly later timescale which locates the mission in the mid-450s and accepts that 493, a traditional date for the saint's death, as recorded in the *Annals of Ulster*, may well be fairly accurate. A few historians go further still, arguing that Patrick's mission took place at the end of the fifth century. If so, this would tend to confirm the view that Palladius' expedition had very little impact, otherwise a basic church framework should have been in place.

Whatever the truth of the matter, it is clear that the conversion of the Irish was a gradual process. The tales of St Patrick ordaining hundreds of bishops, or baptizing seven kings in a single day, are certainly apocryphal. Instead, it is much more likely that paganism and Christianity existed side-by-side for quite some time. Diarmait mac Cerbaill, who ruled as high king from c. 545 to c. 565 (see pp.97–8), is one of several notable figures who coverted to Christianity, but also continued to observe heathen practices.

Paganism and Christianity Side-by-Side

For the pagan Celts, with their polytheistic beliefs, the combination of two religions presented no problem at all. By the same token, the early missionaries tried to ease the transition to Christianity by adapting some of the trappings of the old beliefs. It can be no accident, for

ST PATRICK'S GRAVE, LOUGH CORRIB, COUNTY MAYO (LEFT)
This is one of a number of sites that claim to mark the burial place of the saint, although the actual location is unknown.

KILNASAGGART STONE, COUNTY ARMAGH (RIGHT)
An early Christian pillar-stone in a monastic cemetery. The inscription relates to Ternûc, son of Ciaran (d. 714/16).

Oisín, the son of Fionn mac Cumhaill, has lingered too long in Tír na nOg, the magical Land of Youth. On his return, he finds Ireland a changed place, inhabited by monks and priests, rather than by the knights of the Fianna:

' *Seeing his bewilderment, the people of Glenasmole brought Oisín before St Patrick, confident that he would know what should be done. The holy man treated Oisín kindly and hospitably, offering him food and shelter. Then he tried to explain how Ireland had been transformed during his absence; how Christianity had come to the land and the old gods had withered away. Oisín lamented loudly when he heard these things, remembering all the happy days that he had enjoyed with the Fianna.*

The son of Fionn remained with Patrick and his priests, for he had nowhere else to go. They looked after him, tending to his frail and aching limbs, and trying to console him with the teachings of the Gospel. Oisín listened patiently; but his mind was elsewhere. Until the end of his days he never ceased to yearn for the feasts at Almu, the rousing hunts in the wild forests, and the comradeship of the lost companions of his youth. '

from the Fionn Cycle

ST PATRICK, GLOGHEEN CHURCH, COUNTY TIPPERARY
Although not the first missionary to work in Ireland, Patrick was the most successful, bringing thousands of new converts into the Christian fold.

example, that St Patrick chose to found his principal church at Armagh (*Ard Macha*), close to the remains of Emain Macha, one of the holiest sites in pagan Ireland. Similarly, Patrick and his followers deliberately Christianized the pillar-stones and ogham slabs that had been erected at places of ritual significance by carving crosses on them. In time, these evolved into the distinctive design of the Celtic cross.

The blurring of Christian and pagan boundaries can also be detected in early literary sources. In religious texts, for instance, the accounts of saints' lives were often embroidered with colourful legends that have obvious

pagan overtones. The best-known example concerns St Brigid of Kildare, who shared many of the attributes of Brigit, the goddess of fire, poetry, fertility and other attributes. According to Christian folklore, she grew up in a druid household, was nourished with the milk of Otherworld cows and celebrated her feast-day at the festival of Imbolc. Many of her miracles were related to inexhaustible supplies of food: her cows, it was said, could produce a lake full of milk; and she had the power to turn her bathwater into ale, to provide drink for visiting clerics – precisely the sort of anecdotes that could be associated with a goddess of fertility.

CLONMACNOIS, COUNTY OFFALY
Traditionally founded by St Ciaran, the monastery at Clonmacnois features the finest array of Celtic crosses in Ireland.

'Most Holy, Shining Like the Sun'

The achievements of St Patrick provided a platform for the scores of missionaries who followed in his wake. Many of these were venerated as saints by the early Church, even though their status was frequently not recognized by the papacy. For the sake of convenience, these holy men were sometimes categorized under different headings. One eighth-century manuscript divided the saints into three separate 'orders'. The first consisted of the initial wave of missionaries after St Patrick, most of whom were bishops. They were described as 'most holy, shining like the sun'. The second order included the founders of the many monasteries that sprang up throughout Ireland during the early medieval period; these men were classed as 'very holy, shining like the moon'. Finally came the

Conversely, some of the later mythical tales have a pronounced Christian element. Several stories, for example, relate how individual members of the Fianna survived into the Christian era and met up with St Patrick and his priests. The most notable of these are the *Acallam na Senórach* (Colloquy of the Old Men), in which Cailte mac Rûnáin, Fionn's former steward, regaled the saint with nostalgic tales of his youth and conducted him on a tour of Ireland, showing him the sites of the Fianna's greatest deeds. In later stories Cailte was superseded by Oisín, Fionn's son, who takes shelter with the cleric after returning from his adventures in Tir na nOg.

anchorites and hermits, who settled in remote and lonely places and were revered as 'holy, shining like the stars'.

The legendary status of St Patrick, which continued to increase with every passing generation, has somewhat obscured the true development of the conversion process in Ireland. Later annalists tended to describe most of the early missionaries as protégés of the saint, even though it is far more likely that they operated quite independently. This is particularly true of Secundinus and Auxilius, both of whom were traditionally known as close disciples of St Patrick. Secundinus (or Sechnaill) preached in Meath, where his identity has been preserved in the place-name Dunshaughlin (*Dún Sechnaill*), while Auxilius worked in County Kildare, where his name is commemorated in Killashee (*Cell Auxili*, or 'the Cell of Auxilius'). For all their traditional associations with St Patrick, there is, however, no firm evidence of any link between their missions. Instead, they were most probably continental bishops who may even have been following in the footsteps of Palladius.

Certainly, the earliest part of the conversion process appears to have been modelled on continental practices. The key figures were bishops rather than abbots, just as they were throughout the Christianized parts of the Roman Empire. These bishops were not able to set up individual dioceses, but they did have specific areas of jurisdiction, which were normally identical with the local *tuath*. No doubt there were hopes of establishing a more formal church hierarchy, with the usual complement of bishops, priests and deacons, but events precluded this.

The Two St Ciarans

By and large, only a few sporadic snippets of information have come down to us about the missionary efforts that took place before the mid-sixth century. Among the leading figures were two saints named Ciaran. Ciaran of Saighir (fifth to sixth century) worked among the Osraige and founded the monastery of Seirkieran (now Saighir) in

GALLARUS ORATORY, COUNTY KERRY
This is the most famous of the early Christian boat-shaped oratories. Its creator utilized the corbelling techniques that had been pioneered by Neolithic tomb-builders.

County Offaly, which later became the burial place of the kings of Ossory. Typically, the place appears to have been important in pagan times, for there are reports that the church was built on the site of a sanctuary that housed a perpetual flame. Ciaran of Clonmacnois (c. 512–c. 45) despite his premature death from the plague, achieved even greater prominence than his namesake, founding one of the greatest Irish monasteries, at Clonmacnois, near the banks of the Shannon.

Other pioneers included Ailbe (d. 527?), who was an itinerant preacher in northern Munster. In common with several other early saints, he was said to have spent his final years in the Land of Promise – a semi-pagan compromise between the Otherworld and the Christian Paradise. St Declán was also based in Munster, working among the Déisi people. His chronology is highly confused; some authorities believe that he was active in the early fifth century, before the arrival of St Patrick, while others place him in the following century. He is frequently cited as the founder of the monastery of Ardmore, in County Waterford.

After the middle years of the sixth century, the internal structure of the Irish Church gradually began to change as the break-up of the Roman Empire severed many of its links with the continent and with the papacy. This in turn undermined the fragile episcopal system, which was still in the early stages of its development. The office of bishop survived, but its influence was now eclipsed by that of the abbots, who ran the country's growing network of monasteries.

The Emergence of Monasticism

Monasticism had originated in Egypt, reaching the West by the fourth century. On a personal level, believers felt that they could achieve sanctification by withdrawing from the secular world and dedicating themselves to the twin activities of prayer and toil (*ora et labora*). As a movement, however, monasticism flourished in Ireland because it offered some purely practical advantages. With the diocesan system, there had always been a potential clash of authority between the bishop – a man who stood outside the normal kin-group of the *tuath* – and the local king. Monasteries offered no such threat. They did not lay

claim to specific territorial jurisdiction, and they could maintain close relations with the secular powers. In some instances land was granted to a monastery on the understanding that a member of the *tuath* would be appointed as its head; in time, these posts often became hereditary. The early abbots of Iona, for example, all belonged to the Cenél Conaill. It also made sense for religious houses to ally themselves with one of the principal ruling dynasties, to gain their protection.

After the mid-sixth century the number of monastic foundations multiplied rapidly. Many of these communities were very small – they could be started up by just two people – but they invariably belonged to large and powerful federations. In most cases a form of clientship existed between a mother-church and its various offshoots, even when they were located far from each other. As a result, the sphere of influence (*paruchia*) of these monastic networks could be quite considerable, particularly as they acted independently of any higher Church authority.

A characteristic example of the power of the federations can be seen from the treatment of St Mochuda (also known as St Cárthach, d. 637/8). He came into conflict with the Uí Néill monasteries of Durrow, Clonmacnois and Clonard, after preaching in their domain. Accordingly, in 636, they approached King Blathmac of the Síl nAedo Sláine and prevailed upon him to expel the cleric from their region. Mochuda was forced to comply, retiring to Lismore (County Waterford), where he founded a monastery of his own.

St Enda and St Finnian

It is impossible to know precisely when monasticism was introduced into Ireland, but its ultimate success is usually attributed to two early pioneers, St Enda (d. c. 530) and St Finnian (d. 549). Enda was born in Meath and was a soldier prior to his conversion. He trained at the British monastery of Whithorn (Galloway), before returning to Ireland and founding a number of religious houses. The most notable of these was Inishmore, on the Aran islands, where he established the first major monastic school on Irish soil.

For all his achievements, Enda's reputation was rapidly overshadowed by that of St Finnian. Born in

CARPET-PAGE, *BOOK OF DURROW*
During the Middle Ages designs from
pagan metalwork were adapted for use
in Christian manuscripts.

Columba: Man of Vision

One of the genuine celebrities who trained under Finnian was St Columba (c. 521–97). Baptized as Crimthann, he adopted the name Colum Cille or Columba (literally 'a dove') when he began his ministry. Even before he undertook this work, he was an influential figure. As a member of the powerful Cenél Conaill dynasty, he came from noble stock and could trace his line back to Niall Noígiallach. Accordingly, he was not slow to involve himself in political affairs, acting as a key negotiator at the Convention of Druim Cett (575) and often serving as an intermediary between Dalriada and the Irish kings. In addition, he was a trained bard and did much to save the order from extinction.

The fact that a man of Columba's high social standing chose to enter the Church indicates the considerable prestige that it had come to enjoy by the mid-sixth century. His career also reflects a new air of confidence within the system: the conversion of Ireland was all but complete, and Irish missionaries now felt ready to spread the Word in other lands. After founding a number of monasteries in his homeland (no fewer than thirty-eight are claimed for him), Columba departed for northern Britain in 563. The immediate cause of his departure is controversial – he is said to have sparked off a war, after refusing to return a precious manuscript – but the results were spectacular. He founded a monastery on the island of Iona, close to the Scottish mainland, which would eventually become one of the principal religious centres of the Celtic Church. He also conducted a highly successful missionary expedition, converting Brude, the ruler of the Picts, and consecrating King Aidan of Dalriada in 574.

The Columban federation of monasteries epitomized the great strength and independence of the Celtic Church, and under their founder's leadership the larger houses began to produce a stunning collection of illuminated manuscripts and sacred artefacts. Columba himself had a high reputation as a scribe: the *Cathach* – a sixth-century psalter, thought to be the oldest surviving Irish manuscript – is often believed to be in his hand. Subsequently his monasteries produced the finest of all the Celtic manuscripts, most notably the *Book of Durrow* and the *Book of Kells*.

Leinster, he studied under St Cadoc (fl. early sixth century) in Wales, before settling once more in his native land. Finnian established several new monasteries, the most important of them at Clonard (County Meath). Here, his fame as a teacher soon began to attract pupils from all over Ireland. Hagiographers later claimed that Finnian had as many as 300 disciples, and hailed him as the tutor of the so-called 'Twelve Apostles of Ireland'. This is certainly an exaggeration, for the 'Apostles' included some of the country's most famous saints – among them Columba, Ciaran of Clonmacnois and Brendan the Navigator – some of whom were not even alive during Finnian's time. Nevertheless, Enda was probably the author of the *Penitential of Vinnianus*, the oldest book of its kind to have survived in Ireland (penitentials contained detailed lists of sins, together with the recommended penance).

ST PATRICK'S CONFRONTATION WITH THE HIGH KING

In reality, the conversion of Ireland was a slow, piecemeal affair. The churchmen at Armagh, however, were keen to promote St Patrick's achievements. So, they published a symbolic account of the process, which took the form of a dramatic confrontation between the saint and the pagan high king.

According to this, Patrick arrived in Ireland at Eastertide in 432. On the Sunday he decided to celebrate the occasion by lighting a paschal fire and climbed the Hill of Slane (County Down) in order to do this. Unbeknown to him, however, this viewpoint was visible from the mound of Tara, where Laoghaire (the high king) and his druids were about to conduct their own ceremony. It was the festival of Beltane, which centred around the ritual of lighting a sacred flame. All other fires should have been extinguished at this time, so the sight of Patrick's bonfire filled the pagans with horror. Angrily they climbed into their chariots and rushed to confront him. The saint was unrepentant, of course, and the two sides engaged in a show of spiritual strength. Patrick won this easily, as an unseen force hurled the druids to the ground and turned the sky dark. Laoghaire was suitably impressed and agreed to be baptized.

The Easter Controversy

In purely liturgical matters, the Columban federation also represented a unique form of early Christianity. In its comparative isolation, the Celtic Church had developed a number of distinctive practices that set it apart from mainstream developments in Rome. The most contentious of these concerned the dating of Easter, although there were also debates about the wearing of the tonsure and the merits of the diocesan system. During the course of the seventh century attempts were made to bring Ireland into line with the rest of Christendom. Inevitably, this centred on the Easter controversy, where the Celts claimed to be following the custom of St John. The papacy, however, had long since decided to calculate the date of Easter according to a system devised by Dionysius Exiguus (c. 500–550). This was introduced into Ireland by Sillán (d. 610), abbot of Bangor, and was also the subject of a mission of inquiry which was despatched to Rome in 631. In Britain, the matter was finally resolved at the Synod of Whitby (664), where the Celtic delegates yielded to the authority of the Pope, but in Ireland the dispute dragged on for another fifty years. The south of the country was first to adopt the Roman method, while Armagh championed it in the north. The Columban federation held out the longest, before finally accepting the new system in 716.

If the successors of Columba were obliged to give way on liturgical matters, they still managed to promote other aspects of Celtic Christianity, for Irish monks were at the

forefront of new missionary expeditions to the continent in the sixth and seventh centuries. Here, the leading pioneer was St Columbanus (c. 543–615), an abbot from Leinster. In around 590 he launched a mission to Gaul, where he founded a number of influential monasteries. These included Annegray, which was established in a disused Roman fort, and Luxeuil in the Vosges region. At a later date (c. 613) Columbanus also founded the Italian monastery of Bobbio. At both Luxeuil and Bobbio his monks lived according to the Irish rule, observing its controversial dating of Easter, and he wrote letters to Gregory I and Boniface IV defending this position. More significantly, they also set up high-quality *scriptoria* (workshops), where scribes produced manuscripts in the Celtic style. The quality of these was admired throughout Europe.

A Hermit's Life

Irish monks were renowned for their austere way of life, a trait that they shared with the third 'order' of saints: the anchorites and hermits, who decided to become 'exiles for Christ', withdrawing from the world to lead a life of contemplation. The word 'exile' is no exaggeration for, in the Celtic period, anyone who abandoned their *tuath* lost both their legal and their social identity. The decision to live alone thus represented a genuine act of self-sacrifice.

BEEHIVE HUT, INISHMURRAY ISLAND, COUNTY SLIGO
Many hermits and monks were attracted to Inishmurray, settling at the monastery founded by St Molaise. Island communities were very vulnerable to Viking attacks, however, and this one was snuffed out in the early ninth century.

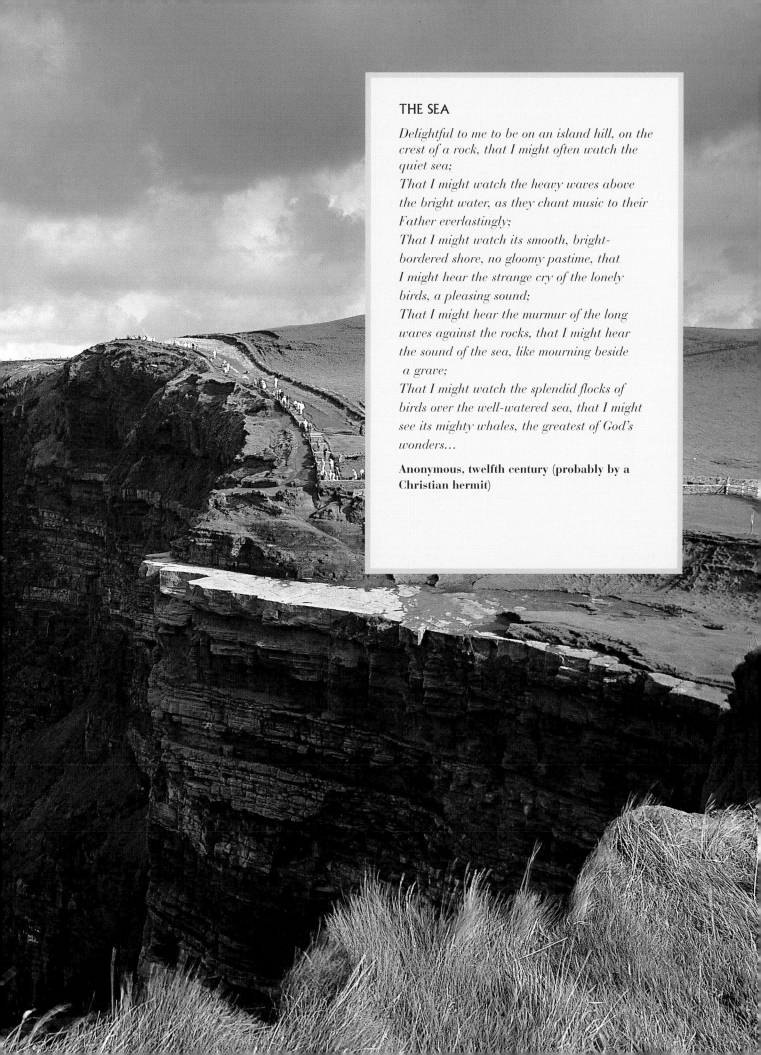

THE SEA

Delightful to me to be on an island hill, on the crest of a rock, that I might often watch the quiet sea;
That I might watch the heavy waves above the bright water, as they chant music to their Father everlastingly;
That I might watch its smooth, bright-bordered shore, no gloomy pastime, that I might hear the strange cry of the lonely birds, a pleasing sound;
That I might hear the murmur of the long waves against the rocks, that I might hear the sound of the sea, like mourning beside a grave;
That I might watch the splendid flocks of birds over the well-watered sea, that I might see its mighty whales, the greatest of God's wonders…

Anonymous, twelfth century (probably by a Christian hermit)

WINTER

I have news for you;
the stag bellows,
winter snows,
summer has gone.

The wind is high and cold,
low is the sun;
its course is brief,
the tide runs high.

Deep and red is the bracken,
its shape is lost;
the wild goose has raised
its customary cry.

Cold has caught
the wings of the birds;
it is the season of ice –
this is my news.

Anonymous, ninth century

This retreat could take a number of forms: sometimes hermits chose to dwell in complete seclusion, seeking a remote spot where they could lead a solitary life; sometimes they gathered in small communities where each man lived in his private cell and had no contact with his fellows, except at mealtimes or during common worship. There were even some anchorites who lived within the bounds of a monastery, obeying its rule, but not communicating with the other monks.

The site of many early hermitages can be gauged from current place-names. The term for this kind of retreat was a *disert* (from the Latin *desertum*), which has given rise to such names as Dysert O'Dea in County Clare, marking the spot where St Tola (d. 737) chose to retire. The prefix *cill*, meaning 'cell', is another helpful indicator. Many hermits also opted to live on tiny islands which were almost inaccessible from the mainland. Traces of early anchoretic communities can still be found on a number of these off the Atlantic coast.

The decision to live as a hermit was not necessarily a lifetime calling. St Finbar (c. 560–c. 610), for example, lived for a time as a hermit at Gougane Barra. Soon, however, his reputation grew and disciples came to join him. Acceding to their wishes, Finbar founded a religious house on the site, which later became famous for its school, and then went on to establish an even greater monastery at Cork.

Cases of this kind were exceptional, though, and most anchorites remained anonymous figures. The most visible signs of their existence can be found not in the written accounts of saints' lives, but in the buildings that they left behind them. Hermits had to erect their own dwelling place and, in the Celtic period, the most typical choice of structure was a form of beehive hut, known as a *clochán*. This was a small drystone building, with a dome-like corbelled roof. Most had tiny entrances and no windows, in order to keep in the warmth, and it is possible that they were originally covered in clods of earth.

Beehive huts were particularly common in the west of the country – the remains of more than 400 huts have been noted in the Dingle peninsula (County Kerry) alone – although some of the most spectacular examples can be found on the island of Skellig Michael. Situated a little way off the Kerry coast, this rocky islet was once home to a small community of hermits, who must have struggled to survive in such a bleak and inhospitable setting.

Celebrating Nature

If nothing else, the exposed and isolated position of many Christian dwellings made their occupants keenly aware of the fickle nature of the elements. Small wonder then that some of the earliest Irish poetry was composed by monks and hermits, whose verses display an acute sensitivity to

PREVIOUS PAGE –
O'BRIEN'S TOWER, CLIFFS OF
MOHER, COUNTY CLARE
The Cliffs of Moher are over 200 metres
(650 feet) tall and form one of the most
dramatic stretches of Ireland's coastline.
The cliffs take their name from an ancient
promontory fort called Mothair.

the beauties of nature, the changing of the seasons, and the calls and signs of native wildlife. The most minute natural phenomena are described with absolute clarity and freshness, as if they were being observed for the very first time. Beyond these visual details, two sentiments are expressed again and again. First, there is a genuine delight in peace, solitude and the ways of the hermit; second, a profound conviction that every single aspect of nature – every blossom, every bird-call, every snowfall – is a reflection of divine beauty and confirmation of God's love for humanity.

However, this spirit of optimism was not maintained throughout the Celtic era. By the eighth century there were signs that some of the ascetic ideals of the early monks and anchorites were starting to wane. This decline has often been blamed on the Viking raids, which tore apart so many religious communities, but the trend had already begun before the onset of these troubles. Nepotism was rife within the monastic community, with posts frequently passing from father to son; and some monasteries even took to the battlefield to protect their material interests. The well-documented clash between the monks of Durrow and Clonmacnois (see p.123) was no isolated case.

Early Irish verse from the margin of a ninth-century manuscript in the library of St Gall, Switzerland

Over me green branches hang
A blackbird leads the loud song
Above my pen-lined booklet I hear a fluting bird-throng.

The cuckoo pipes a clear call
Its dun cloak hid in deep dell:
Praise to God for this goodness
That in woodland I write well.

[Trans. Máire MacNeill, cited in *Ancient Ireland* by Jacqueline O'Brien and Peter Harbison, Weidenfeld & Nicolson, 1996, p.53.]

The 'Companions of God'

The Church made determined efforts to counter these ills. In Ireland, the lead was taken by a new breed of anchorite, the Culdees, who took their name from the Old Irish words *Célé Dé* ('Companions of God'). The Culdees gathered in small groups – often thirteen, in imitation of Christ and the Apostles – and adopted an extremely austere way of life. They also carried out a range of pastoral duties, such as caring for the poor and the sick.

The greatest of the Culdee houses were Tallaght and Finglas, both in County Dublin, which were traditionally known as the 'Two Eyes of Ireland'. Tallaght was founded by St Maelruain (d. 792), who is generally regarded as the driving force behind the Culdee movement. Little is known about his life, although some of his writings have survived, among them the *Rule of the Célé Dé*. Maelruain believed that there were but 'three profitable things in the day: prayer, labour and study', and that 'labour in piety is the most excellent work of all'. Certainly the reputation of his church was immense. When its sanctuary was violated in 811, for instance, the monks of Tallaght persuaded the high king, Aed Oirdnide, to suspend the great assembly at Teltown and intervene in the matter.

Maelruain had a number of important pupils, most notably Máel-Díthruib (d. 840) – who is associated with the monastery of Terryglass in County Tipperary – and Oengus mac Oengobann (d. 824). The latter is now usually known as Oengus the Culdee, and is probably the most celebrated figure in the movement. He was the son of an Ulster king, but chose to live an austere life as a hermit at Dysertenos (literally 'Oengus' retreat'), in County Laois, before joining the community at Tallaght. There he initially concealed both his learning and his royal identity, taking on the most menial of tasks. Eventually Maelruain uncovered the truth and the two men collaborated on a number of religious texts, including the *Martyrology of Tallaght*. Oengus' own writings included the *Festology of Clonenagh* and the *Martyrology of Oengus*, together with a selection of verse.

In many ways, the independent spirit of the Culdees represented the last throes of Celtic Christianity in Ireland. They survived until around the eleventh century, when they were gradually replaced by Canons Regular

MONASTIC DISPUTES

The Irish Church was noted for the ascetic way of life chosen by some of its monks, but it also had a profoundly secular side, which often led to violence. The great monastic houses became extremely wealthy and used every means to safeguard their traditions. Their taste for warfare was stimulated by several important factors. Many abbots were laymen who also ruled over the local tribe, and it was often hard to separate their different functions. In addition, clerics did not become exempt from military service until 804 and were thus all too familiar with military affairs. This was further encouraged by the Brehon Laws (see p.30–3), which stated that in some cases victims should seek their own redress.

The most notorious of the monastic feuds involved the monasteries of Clonmacnois and Durrow. In 753 Domnall Mide of the southern Uí Néill – who had recently become high king – recognized the supremacy of the Columban federation. Accordingly, when he died in 763 Domnall was buried with due pomp at Durrow, one of the leading Columban houses. This enraged the authorities at Clonmacnois, since Domnall's ancestors had traditionally been buried at their monastery. They realized that the loss of this privilege would cost them dearly, in terms of both prestige and revenue, so they fought a pitched battle with the monks at Durrow, during which 200 of the latter were slain.

(later Augustinian Canons). In the meantime, all other impulses for reform stemmed from continental Europe. In Ireland's case, the most significant was the spread of the Cistercian order during the twelfth century, which resulted in the creation of a series of spectacular new churches.

GREY ABBEY, COUNTY DOWN
Founded in 1193 by Affeca, daughter of King Godred of Man, Grey Abbey belonged to the Cistercian order. It was one of the first Gothic churches to be built in Ireland.

The Flowering of Celtic Culture

In material terms, the Christian contribution to Celtic Ireland extended far beyond the field of architecture. The Church produced or commissioned a variety of artefacts from native craftsmen, in which the lingering La Tène style was fused with foreign influences. These sacred objects probably represent the finest achievement of early Irish culture.

Many of the artefacts related to the business of conversion. The most pressing need was for religious texts which the missionaries could use when instructing their new flocks. It might seem that a standard Bible would have been the obvious choice for such a task, but this would not have been a practical proposition, for manuscripts were both slow and expensive to produce. It therefore made sense to use shorter texts. These varied considerably, although the version that gained the greatest popularity was the gospel book. As its name suggests, this consisted principally of the four gospels in the New Testament, together with a certain amount of introductory material.

During their travels, most missionaries preferred to use small-format books, which are now commonly known as 'pocket gospels'. These were written in minuscule script and contained a limited amount of decoration, but were easily transportable. The most celebrated Irish examples include the *Book of Dimma*, the *Book of Armagh* and the *Mulling Gospels*. The *Book of Dimma* is typical of the smaller gospel books. It was produced in the mid-eighth century at St Cronan's monastery in Roscrea, County Tipperary, and is notable mainly for its highly stylized portraits of the Evangelists. The *Book of Armagh* is slightly later, dating from the early ninth century. A note in the text states that the manuscript was written by a scribe named Ferdomnach (d. 845/6), under the supervision of Abbot Torbach.

The *Book of Armagh* was much more than a simple gospel book. In physical terms, it was a compilation of various texts: along with a complete copy of the New Testament, it included a Life of St Martin by Sulpicius

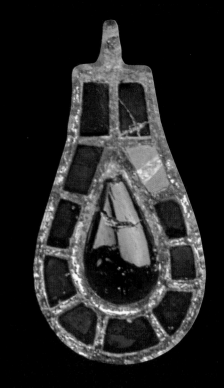

> *The mighty fortress of Tara has perished with the death of her princes; with its army of sages, great Armagh lives on.*
>
> *Boastful Laoghaire's pride is snuffed out – great his misery; the name of Patrick, glorious, famous, is still growing.*
>
> *The Faith has spread and will live on till the Day of Doom; the guilty Gentiles have been carried off and their raths lie abandoned.*
>
> *from the* Martyrology of Oengus the Culdee

Severus (c. 360–c. 420), two key texts by St Patrick (the *Confession* and the *Letter to Coroticus*) and a collection of documents. Beyond this, the book had considerable symbolic value, which was used by the authorities at Armagh to underline their claims to primacy. It was treated with great reverence throughout the Middle Ages, when it was frequently employed on ceremonial occasions and in the swearing of oaths.

The *Mulling Gospels* were said to be a ninth-century copy of the text transcribed by St Moling (d. 697), who founded the monastery of St Mullings (County Carlow) and reputedly went on to become Bishop of Ferns. The book is most famous for its sketch of the ground-plan of St Mulling's, a unique record of the way in which early monasteries were laid out. It is now displayed in an elaborate, jewelled shrine in the library of Trinity College, Dublin.

ITEMS OF JEWELLERY
Surviving Celtic styles left their mark on many European cultures, as these pins, pendant and mount from the first to seventh centuries demonstrate.

SHRINE OF ST PATRICK'S BELL
On this ornate reliquary, dating from
c. 1100, traditional Celtic motifs mingle
with Viking influences.

Gospel Books

As a rule, the type of manuscript that normally attracted such attention was the large-format gospel book, which did not have to fulfil the practical criteria of the smaller texts – it was not used for preaching or for scholarly study and did not need to be portable. Instead, it was placed on prominent public display, in the hope that it would enhance the prestige of the monastery that had produced it.

These larger volumes were a considerable investment on the part of their creators. Materials were extremely expensive: it took the skin of a whole calf or sheep to provide a double sheet of vellum (parchment). By the same calculation, even a modest gospel book required the hides of a sizeable herd, and it has been estimated that the *Book of Kells* involved the slaughter of some 200 animals. In addition, the copying and ornamentation of the manuscript were a slow, painstaking business. The results, however, were spectacular. The most luxurious of the gospel books were lavishly illustrated with portraits of the four Evangelists, elaborate calligraphy and sheets of abstract decoration, which are now known as 'carpet-pages'. The calligraphy and the carpet-pages are particularly interesting, because they reproduced the swirling, hypnotic spiral patterns that had featured extensively on the metalwork of the pagan Celts. As such, they represented a final blossoming of the old La Tène style, which had somehow managed to survive from the Iron Age.

The most celebrated Celtic manuscripts were the *Book of Durrow* and the *Book of Kells*. The former was produced in c. 680 and can justly claim to have pioneered the format of the larger gospel books. It was a treasured possession of the monastery of Durrow (County Offaly), one of St Columba's principal foundations. The *Book of Kells* dates from c. 800 and was probably begun at Iona, at the very time when the place was being beset by Viking raids. Several different artists were involved in its design, and its decoration – the most intricate of any manuscript from this period – displays a number of different influences, including Germanic animal motifs, Byzantine icons and La Tène spirals.

The Irish gospel books were traditionally displayed in a purpose-built box-shrine, known as a *cumdach*. This receptacle was often inlaid with precious metals and jewels, and could be a striking work of art in its own right. Indeed, when the *Book of Kells* was stolen in 1006–7, the thief discarded the illuminated manuscript and made off with the shrine it was displayed in. The very fact that a *cumdach* was used indicates the high esteem in which these books were held. In many cases, they were treated like holy relics, and near-magical powers were ascribed to them.

The Touring of Relics

Relics played a vital role in the early Irish Church, and a varied selection of shrines was designed to hold them. The simplest of these comprised a small, hinged casket, formed in the shape of a house and decorated with enamel inlay. This invariably contained some corporeal remnant of the local saint. Monasteries competed for ownership of these because, in most cases, the governing church in a monastic federation was also the burial place of its founder. Any monastery with a sizeable collection of relics was assured of a high reputation, and could earn extra revenue when the relics were taken round on tour.

Such tours were originally undertaken for the benefit of the entire community. They were carried out at times of general crisis – such as epidemics, famines or outbreaks of cattle sickness – when it was hoped that they might provide either consolation or a cure for the problem in question. One of the earliest recorded instances occurred in 742–3, when the relics of Trian of Kildalkey were transported around part of Meath during a smallpox epidemic. The monks of Clonard performed a similar task in 776, touring with the relics of St Finnian, their founder, during an outbreak of a different disease. As the clerics travelled round with their relics, it became customary for believers to make offerings to the monastery; for this reason, tours were soon being carried out on a more regular basis.

Not all shrines were designed to house bodily remains. Many contained the belongings of founder saints. The most sought-after items were abbatial staffs, which might be cased in precious metal and formed into croziers. These could then be used in church services and processions. Bell-shrines were also popular. The *Annals of Ulster* reported that, in 552, St Columba removed St Patrick's bell – the so-called 'Bell of the Will' – from his tomb, so that it could be used as a relic. It was later placed in an elaborately carved shrine.

Some relics were used for decidedly secular purposes. Most tribes, for example, possessed a *cathach* ('battler') – a memento of their patron saint – which they hoped would bring them good fortune on the battlefield. This was displayed to their warriors amid great ceremony before the fighting began. Traditionally it was borne aloft

THE MACDURNAN GOSPELS

In Celtic manuscripts the gospels were often illustrated with portraits of the relevant Evangelist. This ninth-century figure, with his crozier and book, is St Luke.

by a cleric and carried round the army three times, in a 'sunwise' direction (see also p.95). The relic itself might take many forms, but the most famous example was the *cathach* of the Cenél Conaill, a psalter that was said to have been written by St Columba himself. A *Life* of the saint described how the talisman was displayed at the Battle of Cúldrebene, noting also that it was stored in a silver-gilt shrine, which was never to be unlocked. When the box was finally opened, in the nineteenth century, an ancient manuscript of the Psalms was revealed.

The Celtic Cross

The other great feature of the early Christian era was the rise of Irish stonework, most notably in the form of the Celtic cross. This evolved from the standing stones that pagans had often erected at their holiest ritual sites. When St Patrick and his fellow missionaries arrived in Ireland, they began to transform these into Christian memorials. At first they did nothing more than add a simple cross, but gradually the designs became more inventive, incorporating ideas taken from contemporary metalwork. The stone slabs at Carndonagh and Fahan Mura (both in County Donegal), for example, feature heavily stylized human figures sheltering beneath the carved image of a large cross; this, in typical La Tène fashion, is composed of decorative interlacing and knotwork.

Succeeding generations transcended these early influences. The crosses became taller, sometimes reaching heights of 6 metres (20 feet), and began to feature realistic depictions of biblical scenes. These 'Crosses of the Scriptures' became the focus for outdoor sermons, where the images fulfilled the same didactic function as frescoes or stained-glass windows inside a church. The trend reached its peak during the tenth century, which witnessed the creation of the outstanding crosses at Clonmacnois (County Offaly) and Monasterboice (County Louth).

Irish stone-carving was not restricted to monumental crosses. It can also be found on the tomb-slabs of the period. These are particularly helpful to historians, since they are often dated. One of the most attractive examples commemorates St Berechtir (d. 839), whose grave can be found at Tullylease, in County Cork. Its patterned cross is of considerable interest, because it bears a striking resemblance to the designs of some carpet-pages in contemporary manuscripts.

Decorated grave-slabs have received less attention than the high crosses, because they did not always survive for long. The stones themselves were deemed to have great protective powers and, after a time, they were often broken up and buried in a fresh grave, in the hope that the original 'owner' would intercede for the soul of the newly deceased.

There has been much speculation about the reasons why Irish craftsmen channelled so much of their creative energy into stone-carving. The likeliest theories relate to the durability of the material. The sumptuous metal artefacts that the early Christians had made for their churches were proving a great temptation for foreign marauders. In the great high crosses, at least, believers knew that they had created lasting monuments which could express the strength and permanence of their faith.

MOONE CROSS, COUNTY KILDARE (LEFT)
With its imaginative, stylized scenes, Moone is one of the most striking Irish crosses. The figures on the base, for example, represent the twelve apostles.

NORTH CROSS, CASTLEDERMOT, COUNTY KILDARE (RIGHT)
Later Celtic crosses featured scenes from the Scriptures. The centrepiece here shows Adam and Eve at the Tree of Knowledge.

CHAPTER SEVEN

THE INVADERS

The end of the eighth century saw the start of ferocious raids by the Vikings, who plundered the rich pickings of the Church and moved gradually inland. At the Black Pool (*Dubh Linn*) on the River Liffey the Vikings first established a shipyard and base, which slowly grew in wealth and prosperity as a trading centre. However, native chiefs such as the illustrious high king Brian Boru did not let the Vikings go unchallenged, although the Norsemen did gradually become integrated in Irish society, intermarrying and combining their own distinctive artistic styles with those of Irish craftsmen. But Church reform heralded the demise of Celtic Ireland, as outside influences gathered sway and the Normans seized their chance to conquer the island.

GLENDALOUGH, COUNTY WICKLOW
Round towers served as both lookout posts and refuges during the dark days of the Viking raids.

THE INVADERS

The Coming of the Vikings

By the eighth century the Irish Church had become both powerful and wealthy. The great monastic houses had expanded into miniature cities and their churches resembled treasure stores, glittering with jewelled shrines, silver chalices and sumptuous manuscripts. The abbots who administered these riches doubtless felt secure enough, convinced that the threat of divine retribution would deter any Christian wrongdoers from robbing them, but they were soon to discover that their churches offered a tempting prize for pagan outsiders.

The first signs of trouble appeared at the end of the eighth century, when Ireland, Britain and northern Europe all came under attack from the Vikings at approximately the same time. In 793 the island monastery of Lindisfarne was attacked; two years later Ireland suffered its first raids, as the islands of Rathlin (County Antrim), Inishmurray (County Sligo) and Lambay (County Dublin) were pillaged. The targets of all these attacks were monasteries, and in 798 the religious community on St Patrick's Island (County Dublin) became the next victim; the great Columban church at Iona was one of those hardest hit, with raids in 795, 802

CHALICE AND BROOCH
Ornate Celtic metalwork was greatly prized by the Vikings. The Ardagh Chalice (right) was buried for safe-keeping, while the Tara Brooch (far right) was probably lost during a raid.

and 806, and the monks eventually decided to seek a safer home at the inland monastery of Kells (County Meath). Small wonder that some Christian communities felt that their entire world was caving in. One annalist wrote plaintively of 'the plundering of all the islands of Britain by the pagans'.

The reasons for this sudden onslaught have been much disputed. There have been claims – usually now discounted – that it stemmed from a serious climate change which led the northmen to seek out warmer lands. Equally, there are those who regard it as a consequence of Frankish expansion in the Baltic region, which pushed the native tribespeople out of some of their most fertile territories. More convincing is the theory that the root cause was over-population at home. This was exacerbated by the Vikings' *odal* system of inheritance, which ruled that every son was entitled to a portion of his father's estate. In regions where fertile land was in short supply, this made overseas raids or settlement an attractive proposition. Most of the Vikings who attacked Ireland came from regions of modern-day Norway, where this problem was particularly acute.

In practical terms, the scope for these foreign sorties was increased by the development of the *hafskip*, the remarkable ocean-going longship. With its metres of sail, it was nippy at sea, yet light enough to manoeuvre down rivers or to be carried overland. Above all, it was perfectly designed to glide ashore with great ease, enabling its warriors to carry out their devastating raids with lightning speed, before the locals could organize a proper defence.

Rich Pickings

These hit-and-run attacks set the pattern for the early years of the ninth century. The wanton destruction and bloodshed initiated by the Vikings were vividly portrayed by the annalists, who, as monks themselves, may well have experienced the violence at first hand. Despite this, the frequency of the attacks was comparatively low. There is a sense that the raiders were testing their enemies' strength, scarcely able to believe that such rich pickings could be found at island or coastal sites that were both poorly defended and easily accessible for their ships. They could hardly have understood that the early

BOOTY

One of the most telling proofs of the fear and disruption caused by the Viking raids is the way in which some of the most precious artefacts of the period were preserved. In many cases the find-spot was not an archaeological site in a monastery or a settlement, but a random location where objects were hastily buried and never retrieved. The Tara Brooch – the finest of all the early Irish jewels – provides a typical example. This was discovered in 1850, when a group of boys were playing on the beach at Bettystown, County Meath. Just beneath the surface of the sand they came across a wooden box containing the precious brooch. No one can be sure how it got there, though its proximity to the sea suggests that it may have been placed there for temporary safe-keeping by a Viking raider who never managed to return for it.

Not all finds of this kind would have been booty. Some were probably hoards, buried by fearful owners to prevent their theft. Two of the finest collections of ecclesiastical metalwork may well have been lost in this way. The Ardagh hoard, which included two silver chalices, was discovered in 1868 near the banks of the Shannon, by a young lad digging for potatoes, while the Derrynaflan hoard, with its rich array of liturgical equipment, was found in County Tipperary in 1980. Nobody knows whether these treasures were buried by monks or robbers, but the fact that they were never retrieved is a poignant reminder of the violence and uncertainty of the times.

Christians' desire to become 'exiles for Christ' had led them to locate their churches in areas that were particularly vulnerable to attack.

It is true that the Vikings met with some resistance. In 811 one of the annals recorded a 'slaughter of the heathen by the Ulaid' and, a year later, a similar victory was achieved by the Fir Umaill at Clew Bay (County Mayo). Successes of this kind were few and far between, however, and were often swiftly avenged. The Fir Umaill, for example, were unable to bask in their victory for long, since they went on to suffer a resounding defeat by the Vikings in 813.

Bitter is the wind tonight,
It tosses the ocean's white hair;
This night I do not fear the northmen
Coursing wildly on
the Irish Sea.

Anonymous, ninth century (written in the margin of a manuscript)

Plunder and Ransom

In the 830s the Viking forays entered a new and deadlier phase. The raids became much more frequent and sustained, and now covered a broader area. Hitherto Ulster and Leinster had borne the brunt of the attacks, but in 835 there was widespread looting among the churches of west Munster and, the following year, annalists reported 'a most cruel devastation of all the lands of Connaught by the heathens'. At the same time, the raiders also penetrated inland, pillaging the territory of the southern Uí Néill. As they did so, a shift in tactics became apparent. Instead of simply ransacking monastic sanctuaries, the Norsemen now began to carry off captives, attempting to hold some of the higher-ranking clerics for ransom.

In 837, after several years of plundering in the west, the Vikings turned their attention to the east midlands. Large fleets sailed up the Rivers Boyne and Liffey. Each of these fleets numbered some sixty ships and carried around 3,000 men. With such forces the Vikings ravaged everything that fell in their path – not just monasteries, but also fortresses and farmsteads. In addition they fought a pitched battle with the Uí Néill at the unidentified site of Inber na mBarc, winning a notable victory.

ATHLONE CRUCIFIXION PLAQUE
The tiny holes along the edge of this seventh-century plaque suggest that it was pinned on to board and used as a book cover.

SKELLIG ISLANDS, COUNTY KERRY
Vikings plundered the anchoritic settlements on the Skelligs in 823, though the community remained in existence until the eleventh century.

As the decade wore on, new horrors became evident. Armagh and Kildare – the holiest sites in Ireland – were desecrated for the first time. There was also a growing awareness among the annalists that a significant change was under way. In place of the anonymous war-bands that had been mentioned earlier in the century, the annals now spoke of 'royal' fleets and mentioned individual Viking leaders – names such as Saxoilbh and Turgeis. Worse still, their fleets seemed destined to become a permanent fixture. In 840–1 the Vikings wintered in Ireland for the first time and began to set up bases (*longphorts*), which hinted at the start of a full-scale invasion or, at the very least, permanent staging posts for inland raiding.

The Black Pool

The most important of these bases was established at *Ath Cliath* (Ford of the Hurdles), an ancient crossing of the Liffey, which the northmen had taken in 837. Here, at a spot known as the Black Pool (*Dubh Linn*), they built a rudimentary shipyard in 841 where they could repair and protect their vessels. This consisted of little more than a series of earthen ramparts, but in time the fortified trading town of Dublin would grow up around it.

The ramparts have long since vanished, but one important aspect of the early Viking occupation has been preserved. This is the cemetery of Kilmainham, which was discovered during the nineteenth century, when work was being carried out on the Dublin railway. Sadly, the importance of the find was not realized until much of the graveyard had been destroyed, making it impossible to assess either the original size of the cemetery or the precise context of its many grave-goods. Nevertheless, it is clear that the place had a predominantly military character. The bulk of the finds were weapons, among them forty swords, thirty-five spear-heads and a selection of axes, arrowheads and shield bosses. Alongside these finds archaeologists unearthed several metalworking tools (hammers, tongs, knives) and a number of female graves, containing jewellery or domestic items (brooches, pins, combs).

The settlement at Dublin was no isolated phenomenon. The Vikings set up similar coastal bases at Wexford (*Veigsfjörthr*), Limerick (*Hlymrekr*) and Wicklow

NEWGRANGE, COUNTY MEATH
*Nowhere was safe during the height of the
attacks. In 863 Ivar the Boneless and his
men desecrated the sanctum of Newgrange.*

(*Vikingaló*). The initial motive, undoubtedly, was to provide springboards for inland raids, but there was also a
positive aspect to this development. Irish anchorites had
often chosen to live near the coast, because they wished to
distance themselves from the major centres of power. The
Vikings reversed this trend, deliberately siting their
strongholds close to the sea, so that they could engage in
commercial activities. Dublin, in particular, benefited
from this move. It rapidly grew into a useful trading link
between Scandinavia and continental Europe and, by the
end of the Viking period in around 1014, it had become
a major trading centre.

The development of permanent settlements had other
implications for the invaders. The initial Viking raids had
proved devastating, because of their sheer speed. Internal
communications within Ireland were very poor and this,
coupled with the fact that most tribes remained deeply
involved in their own private squabbles, meant that the
raiders had usually vanished long before any substantial
challenge could be mounted against them. With the presence of a permanent force on Irish soil the enemy was no
longer a moving target. This resulted in a number of
striking successes by the native tribes in the 840s.

Maélsechnaill Wreaks Revenge

Resistance was spearheaded by Maélsechnaill of the
Clann Cholmáin. In 845 he put an end to the plundering
of Turgeis, capturing and drowning the Viking leader at
Lough Owel (County Westmeath). Then, during his reign
as high king (846–62), he slaughtered 700 Vikings at the
Battle of Lough Skreen (848) and, a year later, joined
with the war-lords of Brega in storming the settlement of
Dublin. These successes did not, however, distract
Maélsechnaill from also pursuing traditional dynastic
policies. In 858 his forces ravaged Munster, reaching as
far as the south coast – the first time that an Uí Néill ruler
had been able to achieve this. As a result Munster was
forced to cede the kingdom of Osraige at the royal assembly of Rahugh (County Westmeath) the following year.

Without question, Maélsechnaill was the greatest Irish ruler of the century, and the first to bring genuine substance to the office of high king.

Meanwhile the Norsemen were coming under threat from a different quarter. In 849 Danish ships arrived in Irish waters for the first time, and much of their hostility was vented on their fellow Scandinavians. In 851 the Norse *longphorts* at Dublin and Linns (County Louth) were pillaged. Then, two years later, the rival fleets clashed in a major battle on Carlingford Lough. The fighting raged for three days, before the Norsemen abandoned their ships in total disarray.

Surprisingly, perhaps, the Danes did not consolidate their victory, and it was the Norwegian settlements that survived. Within the space of a few years they had been absorbed into the political landscape and began forging alliances with local Irish factions, in order to protect their interests. Both Cináed mac Conaing, the king of Brega and Knowth, and Cerball mac Dúnlainge of Osraige attempted to curb Maélsechnaill's influence by allying themselves with the Norsemen of Dublin. In Cináed's case, at least, this ended in disaster, when the high king had him drowned in a shallow stream – an execution technique that he had learned from the northmen. Despite this, Irish and Viking alliances soon became a matter of political routine, in which Dublin traditionally sided with Leinster.

The Sacking of Newgrange

Norse fortunes revived in the 860s, when Olaf Guthfrithsson and Ivar the Boneless led their war-bands on a new campaign of terror. Their most infamous act occurred in 863 when, together with a third chieftain named Auisle, they plundered Newgrange and the other megalithic tombs in the Boyne Valley. For centuries, these monuments had been sacrosanct; they had been regarded as gateways to the Otherworld and no one had dared to touch their contents. The atrocity caused genuine outrage and the high king, Aed Findliath (862–79), was swift to take revenge. Lorcan, the Meath king who had guided the northmen to the sanctuary, was blinded on Findliath's orders and, in 866, Findliath's forces destroyed all the Viking strongholds in the north.

For the remainder of the century there was a lull in fighting, largely because the Scandinavians were channelling most of their energies into attacks on England. Irish chieftains took this opportunity to regain lost territories and, for a time, it seemed as if the threat from the north was receding. This optimism reached a peak in 902, when the kings of Brega managed to destroy the settlement of Dublin. The *Annals of Ulster* exulted in their triumph: 'The heathens were driven from Ireland [i.e. Dublin]… and they abandoned a great number of their ships, escaping half-dead after they had been wounded and broken.'

VIKING HELMET
The Norsemen were able to wreak havoc because of their superior weaponry and more effective fighting skills.

These celebrations were premature, for in the second decade of the tenth century the Vikings unleashed a fresh wave of violence against Ireland. In 914 new war-fleets arrived in Waterford, ready to plunder the surrounding countryside. The monasteries of Lismore, Aghaboe and Cork were all sacked, and there was widespread looting in Munster and Leinster. Three years later a new Dublin settlement was founded by Sitriuc, grandson of Imar, and his followers. Niall Glúndub, the high king and chief of the Cenél nEógain, tried to counter this by mustering a combined force, drawn from all the Uí Néill tribes. The two armies clashed at the Battle of Islandbridge (919), where Niall's warriors suffered a resounding defeat. This was to be the last serious threat to Dublin's existence.

The Rise of Dublin

Substantial archaeological remains of the second Viking settlement have survived, and these confirm the northmen's determination to create a permanent township that was unlike any of the earlier communities in Ireland (or, for that matter, any of their towns in Norway). The houses were mostly built to a uniform pattern, with walls of timber and wattle. Some even had a primitive form of cavity insulation. The facilities included a general drainage system and, although the ramparts of Dublin were considerably enlarged, the place became far more than a military base. Many of its inhabitants were merchants or craftsmen, while the surrounding countryside (Dyflinarskiri or Dublinshire) provided space for their crops, cattle and building materials. Dublin's wealth made it a tempting prize for neighbouring chieftains, but there would be no further attempts to destroy it. Instead, local warlords increasingly saw it as a potential source of revenue, and preferred to exact tribute from it.

This pattern was repeated with other Norse settlements in the south and east. Ironically, the very success of the Uí Néill deprived them of such rich pickings. The Cenél nEógain had uprooted all the Viking bases north of Dublin, leaving them in a comparative economic backwater. As the tenth century wore on, the Uí Néill were also hampered by the rise of Uí Briúin Bréifne – a dynastic offshoot of the old Uí Briúin tribe – which drove a wedge

VIKING HEAD, NINTH CENTURY
Irish annalists described the Scandinavian marauders as the heathen gaill, *the men of Lochlainn ('Lakeland') and a 'sea-cast flood of aliens'.*

CASHEL

Perched on its rock, the citadel of Cashel has always excited the imagination of historians and folklorists. Its legendary founder was Corc mac Luigthig. According to tradition, he was inspired to build it after witnessing a vision of a yew bush growing out of a boulder, with angels circling around it. This referred to the Eóganachta, the local ruling dynasty, whose name means 'people born out of the yew'.

In another tale, Corc was sent as a messenger to Pictland, bearing on his shield a secret ogham message which recommended that he should be killed. Fortunately the treacherous ruse was spotted by a former slave, who had previously been rescued by Corc, and he altered the message to ensure a more favourable reception for his benefactor. As a result, Corc's mission to the Pictish king was a great success, and he was given the hand of the eldest daughter.

A later myth tells how St Patrick visited Cashel, in order to convert the pagan King Oenghus. During his baptism the saint accidentally impaled the chief's foot with the sharp point of his crozier, but Oenghus bore this without a murmur. When he noticed the wound, Patrick asked the king why he had not complained, to which Oenghus replied that he thought it was part of the ceremony.

between the two branches of the Uí Néill. This left them ill prepared to deal with a new challenge emerging in the south.

In Munster there was a major shift in the balance of power. The Eóganachta, who for centuries had been the dominant force in the south, went into decline. In 963 they lost the kingship of Munster to Mathgamain mac Cennétig (d. 976), a member of the hitherto obscure Dál Cais tribe. These people, better known as the Dalcassians, were based in eastern Clare, where their chief centres were Killaloe and the fortress of Kincora. Mathgamain was the first of their leaders to achieve any real prominence. He may not be a famous name in Irish history, but he cleared the path for his brother, Brian Boru (d. 1014), who was to become the most illustrious of all the Irish high kings.

Brian Boru: 'Emperor of the Irish'

Brian first came to prominence at the Battle of Solohead, near Tipperary, in 968, when he and his brother routed the Vikings of Limerick and went on to ransack their stronghold. He was also swift to take revenge when Mathgamain was ambushed and killed in 976. He pursued the northmen of Limerick into the monastery of Scattery Island (County Clare), where, despite the fact that they were Christians, he had them put to death. In 978 he seized Cashel and, within a year, was in control of most of the southern territories. This set him on a potential collision course with Maélsechnaill II, who became high king in 980. Their power was fairly evenly balanced, but Brian gradually made headway and, in 997, they finally entered negotiations at Clonfert. At this meeting Leinster and Dublin were ceded to the Munster ruler, as the pair carved up Ireland between them.

The inhabitants of Brian's new acquisitions soon proved rebellious. In 999 he suppressed a joint rising by Leinster and Dublin, defeating their coalition at Gleann Máma, near the Wicklow Mountains. In spite of the agreement made at Clonfert, he pressed on into the north, challenging Maélsechnaill in his own heartlands. In 1002 Brian finally succeeded in wresting the high kingship from his rival. Three years later, in an unprecedented symbolic gesture, he sought to legitimize his action by having it confirmed by the Church. He entered Armagh Cathedral in triumph, placed an offering of 500 grammes (20 ounces) of gold on its high altar and confirmed its primacy over all the churches in Ireland. In return, he persuaded the monks to set down an inscription in the *Book of Armagh*, which proclaimed him *Imperator Scottorum* ('Emperor of the Irish').

Some historians have interpreted Brian's move as the first attempt to create a genuinely national monarchy in Ireland, although this is far from clear. It is quite possible that he visualized only a nominal overlordship, similar to that exercised by the Uí Néill. At any rate, he did not manage to achieve national unity. Several of the northern kings refused to acknowledge him, and he faced continuing rebellions in the south. The most serious of these occurred in 1013, when Leinster and Dublin rose together, bolstered by additional Viking forces from the Western Isles and the Isle of Man.

The Battle at Bull Meadow

Brian and his son marched south and blockaded Dublin for several months, but the decisive clash took place the following year. On Good Friday 1014 the two sides gave battle at Clontarf (literally the 'Bull Meadow'), just outside Dublin. It was a bloody encounter that lasted all day and, although Brian's army was victorious, the losses on both sides were horrendous. Estimates suggest that some 4,000 warriors on Brian's side may have been slain, while his opponents lost 7,000 – a huge tally for this period, when most 'battles' were little more than skirmishes. Brian himself was among the casualties, as were his son and grandson.

The Battle of Clontarf was undoubtedly the most celebrated event in early Irish history, and it rapidly became the subject of highly coloured accounts, both in Ireland and in Norway. Traditionally, Brian was said to have been too old to take part in the actual fighting – he was probably in his seventies by this time – and is supposed to have been stabbed in his tent, while kneeling down piously with a Psalter in his hand.

Subsequent assessments of the battle have proved equally fanciful. For many years Clontarf was viewed as a major landmark in Irish history. The battle was cited as the closing chapter in the Viking age – when the threat from the Norsemen was finally extinguished – and as the apogee of the high kingship. Increasingly, though, historians are revising their thoughts about both of these theories.

THE DEATH OF BRIAN BORU
According to legend, the aged Brian Boru was slain in his tent by a Dane named Brodar, following the victory at Clontarf.

Certainly the battle did not mark any specific watershed in relations with the Vikings. There was no concerted effort to expel them from Irish soil because, by the early years of the eleventh century, they had already integrated successfully into native society. This process had been aided by their conversion to Christianity, together with widespread intermarriage and fosterage, all of which were well advanced by the tenth century. Brian himself took a Norse woman as his wife; indeed, there were even Vikings from Limerick fighting on his side during the conflict.

In terms of the high kingship, Brian Boru's principal achievement lay in the fact that he broke the long monopoly of the Uí Néill, which had been the leading power in Ireland for centuries. If anything, though, the events at Clontarf led to increasing instability. The heavy casualties

suffered on the battlefield, most notably the loss of Brian and his direct descendants, prevented the Dál Cais from establishing a durable ruling dynasty, and they soon faded from the limelight. The reins of power were taken up once more by Maélsechnaill II, whose second term as high king lasted until his death in 1022. However, he was unable to establish his supremacy over Dublin and the other Viking towns and, without this, the Uí Néill did not manage to regain their former dominance. Other kings tried to fill the vacuum, but none was able to emulate Brian Boru's success. Instead, there was a significant increase in local rivalries, which ultimately made life easier for the invading Normans.

The overall effect of the Viking incursions was mixed. The greatest impact, undoubtedly, was felt by the Church. Before the raids began, the monastic communities had been the closest equivalents to townships on the Irish mainland, but the Norse attacks put paid to much of this. The buildings, which were mainly wooden, were burned to the ground; many of the faithful were carried off as slaves; and the shrines and libraries were either looted or destroyed. In spite of this, it is notable that most of the leading religious foundations survived, even though they suffered repeated onslaughts. This may say much for the resilience of the Church, but it has also given rise to the theory that the Vikings deliberately 'harvested' some of the richer monasteries. It has been noted from a study of the annals, for example, that the raids often coincided with local feast-days or festivals when large numbers of people congregated in the monastic grounds, among them traders and stall-holders. These regular gatherings, therefore, provided the Norsemen with an ideal opportunity for slave-taking and looting.

Round Towers

❦

It is notable, too, that the monasteries became much better at defending their property. One of the most important architectural developments of the Viking period was the emergence of the Round Towers. These lofty stone structures served a dual purpose: they provided an invaluable vantage point from which lookouts could survey the surrounding countryside and raise the alarm when trouble threatened; and they acted as storehouses where the monastery's treasures might be placed for safe-keeping, and where the monks themselves might take refuge.

DEVENISH ISLAND, COUNTY FERMANAGH
*Rising to a height of more than 24 metres (80 feet),
the Round Tower at Devenish is one of the most
impressive in Ireland. It has a sculpted cornice,
featuring carved heads and figures.*

The towers had several notable defensive features. The narrow entrances were usually placed some 3 metres (10 feet) above ground level, and access was gained by a ladder, which could be pulled up into the structure. The tower itself had very few openings, to minimize the danger of fiery missiles being hurled inside, for, with their wooden interiors, the shafts would certainly have become death-traps if they had been set ablaze.

As an architectural phenomenon, the Round Towers are peculiar to Ireland. Beyond its shores, only three are known to exist – two in Scotland and one on the Isle of Man. At one time there must have been scores of these towers in Ireland, but only some sixty-five have survived. The finest examples can be found at the monasteries of Glendalough (County Wicklow), Devenish (County Fermanagh) and Scattery Island (County Clare).

Changing Decorative Styles

While the Vikings undoubtedly destroyed many ecclesiastical treasures, they also left a more positive mark on Irish culture, for – as their own artefacts became more readily available – they influenced the style of native Irish craftsmen. The cross-fertilization between these two traditions was made easier by the fact that they had a number of common features: both, for example, were semi-abstract styles which relied heavily on interlacings and stylization.

Particularly in their metalwork, Irish craftsmen began to adapt the three main Scandinavian tendencies of the period – Jellinge, Ringerike and Urnes. The Jellinge form of decoration, which originated in Jutland, consisted mainly of disjointed, ribbon-like beasts, with spirals or foliage in place of their hind legs. This style was already in use in Ireland by the tenth century, and is mainly evident on brooches and other items of jewellery.

In Ringerike patterns, which appeared in the second half of the eleventh century, the stylized animals were replaced by curling swathes of foliage. This was rapidly supplanted by the Urnes style, which takes its name from a wooden church in Norway with elaborate carvings. The

THE CROSS OF CONG
This is one of the finest examples of the Irish Urnes style. The openwork panels are decorated with S-shaped ribbon-creatures, while the cross itself, dating from c. 1125, is clamped between the jaws of a ferocious beast.

basic motif was a four-legged beast, intertwined with ribbon-serpents and a maze of tendrils. This produced the same hypnotic effect as the ancient La Tène style, and it was employed on some of the finest church equipment of the period. Some of the most spectacular examples are the Clonmacnois Crozier and the Cross of Cong, both of which are now housed in the National Museum of Ireland in Dublin.

New Trade, New Skills

Outside ecclesiastical matters, the principal impact of the Vikings was on commercial affairs. Their settlements on the east coast soon became important trading centres, linking the Scandinavian homelands with merchants in Britain, Europe and beyond. The main commodities involved were wine, silver and wool, which the Vikings exchanged for fur, ivory and slaves. Fragments of silk have also been discovered, suggesting that their trading network extended a long way to the east. On the most fundamental level of all, the Vikings even introduced a new system of coinage.

In addition to these mercantile interests, they passed on a variety of new skills. Irish borrowings from Norse words indicate that native craftsmen learned much about different techniques in ship-building from the newcomers. Their kings began to make greater use of fleets in their war-like activities, often adopting the tactics and strategies that had been employed against them in the past. Other borrowed terms relate to the physical structure of the new towns or to the actual business of trading – the Irish words for 'window', 'garden', 'hall', 'street' and 'market' all derive from Scandinavian sources. On the debit side, the coastal towns were to provide ideal bases for the Norman invaders when they arrived in Ireland in the twelfth century.

One response that the Viking invasions failed to engender was a sense of national unity. Throughout the period of the raids, resistance was hampered by lack of cooperation between the various rival kingships and, if anything, the situation deteriorated in the century and a half that separated the Battle of Clontarf from the Normans' first appearance.

The lack of stability is most evident in the rapidly shifting fortunes of the leading dynasties. After the death of Maélsechnaill II in 1022, the Uí Néill fell from power and the dominant figure was a king of Leinster, Diarmait mac Mael na mBó (d. 1072). He took the Viking towns of Dublin and Wexford, which gave him control over the lucrative trade with Bristol. However, he never managed to obtain the high kingship, though one of the annals described him rather grandly as 'King of the Britons and the Isles, and of Dublin and the Southern Half of Ireland'. During his reign the Dublin fleet saw action in the Welsh wars and in the Hebrides, while his realm became a refuge for the defeated followers of King Harold after the Norman conquest of England in 1066.

GRIANÁN OF AILEACH, COUNTY DONEGAL
In 1088 this ancient fortress was largely destroyed during a revenge attack by Muirchertach O'Brien.

The Rise of the O'Briens

After Diarmait's death at the Battle of Odba (possibly at Navan, County Meath), the reins of power passed to the descendants of Brian Boru – or the O'Briens, as they were now becoming known. Turlough O'Brien (d. 1086) enjoyed only limited influence beyond his Munster kingdom, although the annalists referred to him euphemistically as *rí Erenn co fressabra* ('king of Ireland, with opposition'). Nevertheless, he established a useful power base for his son, Muirchertach, whom he installed as king of Dublin after subduing Leinster, neutralizing any threat from Meath by dividing it up between competing factions. Turlough also pursued a similar policy in Connacht, where he exploited the bitter rivalry between the O'Rourkes, the O'Connors and the O'Flahertys. The ploy succeeded only too well, although it laid open the door for other alliances with outside parties, which would pose a problem in the future. Turlough did not campaign much in the north, but his reputation made him a respected figure there and several members of the Ulaid travelled to Munster, to seek his support against their enemies.

Turlough was eventually succeeded by Muirchertach (d. 1119), who laid claim to the high kingship from

1086. He adopted a more aggressive approach towards his rivals, swayed perhaps by an early setback in his reign. For in 1088 a combined army of the O'Connors and the O'Loughlins penetrated deep into Munster, setting fire to Limerick and destroying the O'Brien stronghold of Kincora. In due course Muirchertach exacted his revenge. During the early 1090s he concentrated on imposing his will upon the O'Connors and the O'Flahertys of Connacht, before challenging the power of the Cenél nEógain in the north. Here, his chief rival was the redoubtable Domnall O'Loughlin (d. 1121). Between 1097 and 1113 Muirchertach launched no fewer than ten separate campaigns against his enemy, and in one of them (1102) managed to raze the royal seat of Aileach to the ground. An entry in the *Annals of the Four Masters* emphasized the punitive nature of this expedition:

> *Murtagh O'Brien, King of Munster... demolished the Grianán of Aileach, in revenge for the destruction of Kincora... and he ordered his army to bring from Aileach to Limerick a stone of the demolished building for every item of provisions which they had with them.*

Muirchertach sustained his power by making shrewd foreign alliances and marriage pacts. When it appeared that the Norwegian ruler Magnus Barelegs (d. 1103) was about to launch a new series of raids against Ireland, Muirchertach staved them off by marrying one of his daughters to the king's son, Sigurd. Similarly he matched another daughter with Arnulf de Montgomery, brother to the rebellious Earl of Shrewsbury, who was trying to dislodge Henry I from the English throne. Muirchertach sent ships to aid him, but the uprising was eventually quelled.

In Ireland, meanwhile, he suffered his most serious defeat at the Battle of Mag Coba (County Down), where O'Loughlin managed to ransack the king's pavilion and make off with the royal standard. After this there was

MELLIFONT ABBEY, COUNTY LOUTH
Founded by St Malachy in 1142, Mellifont was the first Cistercian abbey in Ireland. The style of its architecture demonstrates the country's growing links with the continent.

stalemate in the north until 1114, when Muirchertach lost the kingship of Munster through illness. He battled to regain his throne, but the balance of power within Ireland as a whole was already shifting away from the O'Briens.

In the eyes of posterity, Muirchertach's most famous deed has nothing to do with his many campaigns, but is linked with an apparent act of generosity. At the Synod of Cashel in 1101 he donated the Rock of Cashel to the Irish Church. The gift was probably politically motivated – the site was the traditional stronghold of his rivals, the MacCarthys – but it has come to be regarded as one of the landmarks of the ecclesiastical reform movement, which transformed Ireland in the eleventh and twelfth centuries.

Church Reform

The Irish Church had been at the forefront of new developments during the early Celtic period, but by the eleventh century it seemed archaic to the authorities at Rome. It was heavily dominated by laymen; its power was still concentrated in the hands of abbots, rather than bishops; its version of the diocesan system was antiquated; and there were as yet no parishes. All this presented an irresistible challenge to two of the most enthusiastic papal reformers of the period, Gregory VII (c. 1020–85) and Urban II (c. 1035–99).

The first hints of change had come earlier in the century, when Sitric, the Norse king of Dublin, decided to found a cathedral (now known as Christ Church). This required the consecration of a new bishop, but Sitric was reluctant to call on one of the Irish monasteries, since these were usually under the sway of a local chief. Instead, he asked the Archbishop of Canterbury to officiate. This may have been the answer to Sitric's immediate problem, but it opened the way to interference from external sources.

This 'interference' came in the form of two Italian-born archbishops of Canterbury – Lanfranc (c. 1005–89) and St Anselm (1033–1109) – who were keen to use their influence to raise the subject of reform. Lanfranc wrote to Turlough O'Brien complaining about a number of abuses (including the Irish practice of divorce), while it was Anselm who persuaded Muirchertach to preside over the Synod of Cashel.

In all, there were three major synods dealing with reform: namely those at Cashel (1101), Rath Breasail (1111) and Kells-Mellifont (1152). They tackled a variety of issues, among them the sale of church benefices, the regulation of marriage, the removal of disproportionate lay influence and the creation of a powerful new system of bishoprics. These were to be administered by four archbishoprics: Armagh, Cashel, Dublin and Tuam.

The reforms brought Ireland into much closer contact with European practice, though at considerable cost to its own culture. For, as the influence of the bishops grew, so the great monastic houses declined. On the one hand, their jurisdiction diminished greatly; on the other, they had to compete with an influx of new monastic orders from the continent – Augustinians, Benedictines and Cistercians all made their appearance on Irish soil.

Artistic Masterpieces

On a positive note, the European orders began to build a magnificent series of new churches, which were far grander than any previously seen in Ireland. The trend was initiated at Cashel, where Cormac MacCarthy commissioned a fine Romanesque chapel (1127–34) for the Benedictine monks. Other masterpieces in this style include the sculpted arcading at Ardmore Cathedral (County Waterford), the great west door at Clonfert Cathedral (County Galway) and the glorious carvings at Tuam Cathedral (County Galway).

The older monasteries were still producing some superb metalwork – the Cross of Cong, the Clonmacnois Crozier and the shrine of St Lachtin's arm all date from this period – but their status was being undermined. The great monastic schools lost their impetus and most scholars moved out. Ironically, this coincided with the preservation of many Irish legends in the Book of the Dun Cow and the Book of Leinster. It was as if the scribes were aware that an important link with the past was being lost.

If the Church reforms heralded the end of early Celtic Ireland, the *coup de grâce* was not far behind. There seemed no obvious sign of this, however, as the O'Connor dynasty of Connacht rose to power. Turlough O'Connor (d. 1156) achieved considerable success during his lengthy reign, largely due to his careful attention to military detail. He constructed a ring of forts in Connacht to protect his rear, as well as a series of strategic bridges across the Shannon. He also maintained a sizeable army and navy, which saw frequent service. He crushed the forces of Munster, partitioning the kingdom into Desmond (south Munster) and Thomond (north Munster), and followed a similar policy in Meath.

For much of his reign Turlough seemed invincible, a genuine contender for the office of a national high king, but in the 1140s Muirchertach mac Lochlainn (d. 1166) of the Uí Néill rose to challenge him. After Turlough's death, he assumed power and a dangerous set of allegiances took shape. Muirchertach sided with Dermot mac Murrough, the king of Leinster, while Turlough's son, Rory, teamed up with Tigernán O'Rourke, the ruler of Bréifne. This precarious stand-off remained in operation until 1166, when a gratuitous act of brutality (the blinding of an Ulaid chief) led to violent reprisals. Muirchertach was killed in battle and Dermot was deposed. Like a house of cards, the political stability of Ireland collapsed in an instant.

The Normans Arrive

Dermot fled to England, where he appealed to Henry II (1133–89) for help. The English king had considered an invasion of Ireland in the mid-1150s and, to this end, had

ARDMORE, COUNTY WATERFORD
*Founded by St Declan, the ruined
church at Ardmore is notable for its
Romanesque arcading.*

already obtained papal permission for the venture, citing the consolidation of Church reforms as his pretext. Accordingly, he allowed Dermot to recruit volunteers to help him recapture his crown. The majority of these came from south Wales and were headed by Richard de Clare (d. 1176), better known by his nickname 'Strongbow'.

The first trickle of Normans arrived in Ireland in 1167, followed by a larger force two years later. From the start, they were spectacularly successful. In 1170 Strongbow stormed into Waterford, and captured Dublin soon afterwards. Following the death of Dermot in 1171, he became the leader of the Anglo-Normans, who continued with their conquest. Strongbow's rapid rise alarmed Henry II, who launched his own expedition in September 1171, in order to establish his supremacy. This was formalized at the Treaty of Windsor (1175), in which Henry claimed Meath and Leinster, along with the towns of Dublin, Waterford and Wexford, while recognizing Rory O'Connor's overlordship of the remainder of Ireland.

Even now, Rory's humiliation was not complete. The conditions of the treaty were breached almost immediately, as the Norman adventurers ignored the specified boundaries. Powerless to stop them, Rory attracted increasing hostility from his own people and was forced to abdicate in 1183. He then retired to the monastery of Cong, where he spent most of his remaining years. When he died there in 1198, the last of the Irish high kings, he was a forgotten man.

The coming of the Normans changed Ireland for ever. With their rigid, feudal outlook they brought the country firmly into line with European developments, sweeping aside more than 1,000 years of Celtic culture. The laws, the legends and the unique artistic traditions of ancient Ireland were all submerged beneath the new foreign influences, although they were never forgotten. The Celtic Revival of the late nineteenth century brought them to the surface once again, reawakening Irish pride in the nation's glorious beginnings.

TRIM CASTLE, COUNTY MEATH
The invading Normans built castles to consolidate their power. Trim was the stronghold of Hugh de Lacy.

Glossary

Beltane Ancient Celtic festival, held on 1 May

Brian Boru The greatest of the Irish high kings, famed for his victory at the Battle of Clontarf (1014)

cashel A prehistoric stone fort

Cattle Raid of Cooley English title of the *Táin Bó Cuailgne*

chape A small metal case, covering the tip of a scabbard

cist A single, box-shaped tomb, made of stone slabs

clochán A beehive hut

cóiced Literally 'a fifth'; used to describe one of the five ancient provinces of Ireland

Conchobar Mythical king of Ulster; a prominent character in the *Táin*

Conn Cétchathach 'Conn of the Hundred Battles'; a legendary Irish king, the grandfather of Cormac mac Airt

Cormac mac Airt Legendary Irish king, the first to rule at Tara

crannog A fortified dwelling, constructed on an artificial island

Cú Chulainn The greatest of the warrior-heroes in early Irish literature; he championed the Ulster cause in the *Táin*

Culdee Order of monks, noted for the austerity of their rule

cumdach A box-shrine for early religious manuscripts, especially gospel books

the Dagda In the Irish pantheon, the father of the gods

Dowris phase A phase in the Irish Bronze Age, named after a hoard discovered in County Offaly

Emain Macha In Irish legend, the ancient capital of Ulster; now identified with Navan Fort, near Armagh

the Fianna A legendary war-band, led by Fionn mac Cumhaill; sometimes cited as a prototype for the Arthurian Knights of the Round Table

Fionn Cycle A group of early stories centred on the exploits of Fionn mac Cumhaill

Fionn mac Cumhaill A warrior-hero in early Irish literature; the leader of the Fianna

Fir Bolg A mythical race of invaders, said to have occupied Ireland before the arrival of the Gaels

Fomorians In Irish legend, an evil race of pirates

gallery-grave A chamber tomb, displaying no distinction between the entrance passage and the burial area

geis A form of taboo

Goidels A race of invaders, who brought the Gaelic language to Ireland; sometimes called 'the Féni'

Hallstatt An Iron Age period named after a cemetery in Austria

Imbolc Ancient Celtic festival, held on 1 February

interglacial A warm interlude between ice ages

Laigin An ancient Celtic race who settled in Leinster

Larnian A Mesolithic culture named after Larne, County Antrim

La Tène An Iron Age period, named after a ritual site in Switzerland

longphorts Early Viking bases

Lugh Celtic sun-god; renowned in Ireland as the foster-father of Cú Chulainn

Lughnasadh Ancient Celtic festival, held on 1 August

Maeve Irish goddess of sovereignty; in the *Táin* she was the warrior-queen of Connacht

microlith A tiny prehistoric tool, often consisting of a single blade, just a few centimetres long

midden A refuse heap in a prehistoric settlement, often containing food remains or fragments of artefacts

Mide Literally 'the middle', this was one of the five ancient provinces of Ireland

Milesians An ancient race of invaders, the fictionalized equivalent of the Goidels

Nemedians According to legend, one of the earliest peoples to inhabit Ireland

Newgrange A megalithic tomb near the River Boyne, Ireland's most famous prehistoric monument

Niall Noígiallach Literally 'Niall of the Nine Hostages', acclaimed as the ancestor of the Uí Néill dynasty

ogham The earliest form of Irish writing

Otherworld A supernatural realm, linked to Celtic concepts of the afterlife

passage-grave A megalithic tomb, usually consisting of a narrow entrance passage and a large burial chamber covered with a mound

Picts Literally 'the painted ones'; an early Celtic people best known for their links with Scotland, although also present in Ireland

Samhain Ancient Celtic festival, held on 1 November

sídhe Fairy mounds; in Irish legend, these were believed to be the dwelling places of the ancient gods

souterrain In prehistoric times, an underground dwelling or storage space, usually built with stone slabs

Strongbow Nickname of Richard de Clare, 2nd Earl of Pembroke (c. 1130–76), the most famous of the Anglo-Norman adventurers

tang A narrow projection at the base of a blade, designed to secure it to a haft

Táin Bó Cuailgne The chief tale of the Ulster Cycle, which recounts the theft of the magical bull of Cooley

Tara A prehistoric site in County Meath, famed as the seat of the Irish high kings

Tir na nOg In Irish legend, the fabulous Land of Youth, where sickness and old age were unknown

torc A metal collar worn by the Celts; often a high-status object with ritual associations

tuath The basic territorial unit in ancient Ireland

Tuatha Dé Danaan The ancient gods of Ireland, sometimes known as 'the Ever-Living Ones'

Uí Néill A powerful Ulster dynasty, claiming descent from Niall Noígiallach

Ulaid An ancient Irish people, who gave their name to the province of Ulster

Ulster Cycle A group of tales, centred on the *Táin*, recounting the exploits of Cú Chulainn and his fellow Ulstermen

Urnfield A Bronze Age culture, taking its name from the practice of burying cremated remains in distinctive urns

Bibliography

Berresford-Ellis, Peter, *Dictionary of Celtic Mythology*, Constable & Co., 1992

Byrne, Francis John, *Irish Kings and High Kings*, Batsford, 1973

Carr-Gomm, Philip, *The Druid Tradition*, Element Books, 1991

Connolly, S.J., ed., *The Oxford Companion to Irish History*, Oxford University Press, 1998

Cross, F.L., ed., *The Oxford Dictionary of the Christian Church*, Oxford University Press, 1974

Dames, Michael, *Mythic Ireland*, Thames & Hudson, undated

Dillon, Myles & Chadwick, Nora, *The Celtic Realms*, Weidenfeld & Nicolson, 1967

Farmer, David Hugh, *The Oxford Dictionary of Saints*, Oxford University Press, 1978

Finlay, Ian, *Celtic Art*, Faber & Faber, 1973

Foster, R.F., *The Oxford Illustrated History of Ireland*, Oxford University Press, 1989

Green, Miranda, *Dictionary of Celtic Myth and Legend*, Thames & Hudson, 1992

Harbison, Peter, *Pre-Christian Ireland*, Thames & Hudson, 1988

Herity, Michael & Eogan, George, *Ireland in History*, Routledge & Kegan Paul, 1977

Joyce P.W., *A Smaller Social History of Ancient Ireland*, Longmans, Green & Co., 1908

Killanin, Lord & Duignan, Michael V., *The Shell Guide to Ireland*, Ebury Press, 1962

MacKillop, James, *Dictionary of Celtic Mythology*, Oxford University Press, 1998

Marsden, John, *The Fury of the Northmen*, St Martin's Press, 1993

Megaw, Ruth & Vincent, *Celtic Art*, Thames & Hudson, 1989

Metropolitan Museum of Art, *Treasures of Early Irish Art 1500 BC to AD 1500*, exhibition catalogue, 1977

Niocaill, Gearóid mac, *Ireland before the Vikings*, Gill & Macmillan, 1972

O'Brien, Jacqueline & Harbison, Peter, *Ancient Ireland*, Weidenfeld & Nicolson, 1996

O Cróinín, D., *Early Medieval Ireland*, Longmans, 1995

O'Kelly, Michael, *Early Ireland*, Cambridge University Press, 1989

Piggott, Stuart, *The Druids*, Thames & Hudson, 1968

Raftery, Barry, *Pagan Celtic Ireland*, Thames & Hudson, 1994

Index

Acknowledgments

I am very grateful for all the support and advice that I have received from friends and colleagues. In particular, I would like to express my thanks to Ian Chilvers, Caroline Juler, Michael Jacobs, Sarah and Emerson Peart and Dominique Zazcek.

Picture Credits